# INTERNATIONAL Hotel AND Resort DESIGN 2

## Wendy Black

HOTELS
&RESTAURANTS INTERNATIONAL

**Library of Applied Design**

*An Imprint of*

P B C   I N T E R N A T I O N A L ,   I N C.   ✦   N E W   Y O R K

Distributor to the book trade in the United States and Canada:

**Rizzoli International Publications Inc.**
300 Park Avenue South
New York, NY 10010


Distributor to the art trade in the United States and Canada:

**PBC International, Inc.**
One School Street
Glen Cove, NY 11542
1-800-527-2826
Fax 516-676-2738


Distributed throughout the rest of the world:

**Hearst Books International**
1350 Avenue of the Americas
New York, NY 10019

Library of Congress Cataloging-in-Publication Data

Black, Wendy
    International hotel and resort design 2 / by Wendy Black
        p. cm.
    Includes index.
    ISBN 0-86636-144-8
    1. Hotels, taverns, etc. 2. Resort architecture. I. Title
NA7800.85 1991
728'.5--dc20                                              91-38023
                                                               CIP

CAVEAT — Information in this text is believed accurate, and will
pose no problem for the student or the casual reader.
However, the author was often constrained by information
contained in signed release forms, information that could
have been in error or not included at all. Any misinformation
(or lack of information) is the result of failure in these
attestations. The author has done whatever is possible to
insure accuracy.

Color separation, printing and binding by
Toppan Printing Co. (H.K.) Ltd. Hong Kong

Typography by
Toledo Typesetting

Printed in Hong Kong

10 9 8 7 6 5 4 3 2 1

# Acknowledgments

Many thanks and deepest gratitude must be given to those who made this book a reality. First to Kevin Clark for being such a patient and encouraging editor, to Don Locke, publisher and James Carper, editor in chief of HOTELS magazine for the opportunity and much of the information needed to produce this book. Also, to the many talented architects, designers and hoteliers a genuine thank you for providing the wonderful properties that grace these pages.

And finally, to my husband Will Rodgers and my sons Hunter and Wyatt who graciously gave me time to do this and to my friends who encouraged me and supported me.

# Table of Contents

# FOREWORD

**James D. Carper,** Editor in Chief, *Hotels*

Talk to seasoned business travelers and they will tell you two things: First, they are tired of look-alike hotels. Second, they want to feel at home when they are on the road.

Talk to hoteliers, and they will tell you two things: First, the competition for the traveler is fierce. Second, these hotel operators also are tired of look-alike hotels.

Those are the twin challenges of hotel designers today; make the hotel comfortable (that's the nature of the hotel business), and make the hotel different from all the other properties on the market (that's the nature of business).

As you turn the pages, you will see that the hotels selected for this book are definitely not look alike—even when the design firm is the same. These photographs represent state-of-the-art hotel designs that are the creations of innovative architecture and interior design firms. This hotel portfolio represents the best in commercial business hotels, destination resorts and boutique properties. They represent all regions of the world. And this collection of hotels shows both newly built and remodeled properties.

Hotels, of course, must shelter and comfort travelers, whether they are away on business or for leisure. While a comfortable bed and warm blankets take care of physical needs, the design can take care of travelers' psychological needs by creating a pleasing, non-threatening and inviting environment—whether for one night or for an extended stay.

In many parts of the world today, the customer has the advantage over the hotelier. In many cities, travelers have an abundance of hotels to choose from. Hotel operators can do much in the way of delivering high-quality service to ensure that guests return. But the design of a hotel itself plays a large role in making guests comfortable and thus likely to return.

A traveler who already has come 2,000 miles still faces one more leg of the journey—that from the front door of the hotel to the front desk, from the lobby to the elevator, up the elevator, down the corridor and at last, to the guestroom—truly the journey's end. Design should make the last trip comfortable, educational and fun. And in more and more hotels, this particular journey is becoming fun and educational.

Designers today are conscious of designing for the local environment. Thus, a vacationer in a new Hawaiian hotel truly feels he or she is on a Polynesian island, not in an all-purpose, generic hotel. Similarly, the traveler to Paris wants to be reminded—designers use subtle touches such as color, artwork, moldings or furnishings—that he is in France. And the skier in the Rocky Mountains wants to be reminded that she is in cowboy country.

A fact of life today is that hotel owners are calling for efficiency—in energy consumption, in employee productivity and in efficient use of space. Thus, some hotel owners are building or renovating lobby space so that it can function not only as a gathering spot, but also as a cocktail lounge and as dining space (especially for breakfasts). Guest rooms must often function as meeting rooms, offices and dining rooms. (Such is the challenge of all-suite hotels.)

Ballrooms must function as classrooms, banquet rooms and nightclubs. Restaurants must often perform triple duty—for breakfast, luncheon and dinner. (Not every hotel operator can afford to maintain a room strictly for dinner service.) And more and more, a hotel as a whole must function as a business center during the week, then as a resort on the weekends when travelers decide to turn a business trip into a mini-vacation. Even resort hotels find that a little meeting space can add occupancy points by attracting extra business.

To the well-traveled reader, this book will trigger some memories of places visited. To the armchair traveler, this book might be the catalyst for on-site inspection. To both readers, I wish you a pleasant journey. Bon voyage!

# Introduction

As all things in life seem to run in cycles, so goes the state of the hotel industry. In the decade of the '80s, the theme for hotels was opulence and grand style. The economy was booming, especially the real estate market, and bankers were handing out money for development. It seemed that well-connected hoteliers were emerging from the casegoods with fists full of money to invest in the industry. Hotel design became a function of ego and thus sprung the newest of the overnight experience, the fantasy hotel — playing on the "Disneyland for adults" concept.

But all the decadence of the '80s gave way to a more conservative new era for the lodging industry. Having suffered from the economic devastation of real estate in the past decade, bankers are still reeling. Banks are no longer banks — just try to borrow money for new hotel construction or refurbishment.

This dramatic change became evident with the development of this book. As the second in the series on international hotel design, it would clearly be a bit more challenging to ferret out more wonderful hotels that were not included in the first book. But the task was a bit more arduous than imagined. The reality is that there is very little new construction, some refurbishments and much more redecorating than face-lifting. Aesthetic makeovers appear to be the trend.

However that doesn't mean that there aren't fabulous and creatively styled hotels around. It just means that they are harder to find. Fewer have unlimited budgets, but even one project in Australia boasts unlimited funds. What this means for architects and designers is that they need to become even more creative in the design approach. That is evident in this book.

As illustrated in these pages, there are some very interesting places to stay around the world. If there is a style trend within these properties, it would be the lean toward Old-World style and details. The use of new materials made to look weathered and old, the use of natural materials that have been in use for centuries and most of all, the employment of artisans and craftspersons for that handmade, one of a kind look.

The overscaled California look is still around, but now the fabrics would be richer — maybe with rich silks and tapestries, and the colors would be richer or more muted. Real antique details, accents and accessories complete the ambience.

But the hotel themes featured in this book run the gamut from hotels built on top of existing New York theaters to a centuries-old wall crumbling in the atrium of a contemporary European property. One other theme becomes evident throughout the pages of this book. The classic concept of beauty becomes challenged and innovation takes precedence. Because hotels are probably the most public locations to experience design, they tend to set the standard for what constitutes good design and usually good taste. However, some of the properties featured here are more examples of interesting or creative solutions. All of them are, however, worth the experience.

One thing to keep in mind as the reader travels through these pages — not every great hotel property has been featured here. Some may have been featured in the first book and still others don't possess the calibre of photography needed to be included. And others, while wonderful, are probably hidden in the shadows of some of the more famous greats. Whatever the case, the hotel industry continues to grow and develop creating fodder for, most probably, another book.

Safe travels to all.

Wendy Black

# The Hotel Beau Rivage

*GENEVA, SWITZERLAND*

When a Grand Dame as venerable as Geneva's Beau Rivage is ready for a face-lift, skilled craftsmanship with an eye toward history is in order. Such was the challenge for interior designer Leila Corbett who completed the task with the style and perfection that the lady deserved. The result is the elegant Five Star hotel just a stone's throw from beautiful Lake Geneva.

The total renovation took only six months to complete and posed its share of challenges. While the hotel was kept in operation, the design team was careful not to disrupt the first class guests who came to enjoy the ambience of the property. During the renovation, the cocktail bar was relocated as were parts of the main lobby. With the hotel steeped in great history as the oldest in Geneva dating back to 1865, the object was to improve the best features while keeping the style as it was originally intended. To that end, all the original cornices, flooring, paneling and plaster work was used—only to be replaced when absolutely necessary.

The 16 foot high ceilings show off the lush draperies and beautiful plaster work which has been carefully restored during the latest remodeling.

**C**raftsmanship is evident throughout the remodeling, particularly with special paint finishes including: marbleizing, faux stone and Trompe L'oeil. All drapery and window coverings were kept in style using swags and tails—some 16 feet high. Carpet design and colors were co-ordinated with the original colors used in the lobby.

Throughout its almost 13 decade history, this hotel has undergone many transformations. But the objective has always been to keep its style and remain absolutely tied to the past century—not just to remain a beautiful hotel museum. Geneva's Beau Rivage has and always will be marked by its beautiful ambience and high quality of services offered with the greatest discretion.

ARCHITECTURE
*Brunischoltz*
INTERIOR DESIGN
*Leila Corbett Limited*
PHOTOGRAPHY
*Michael Dunne*

The Louis XV furniture is in style with the history of this venerable hotel property.

# Berkeley Hotel

*RICHMOND, VIRGINIA, USA*

The designers of this cozy hotel had the challenge of taking a structure that was originally designed as an office building and make it into an elegant, timeless hotel. One of the most difficult feats was to create guestrooms out of an erratic column layout.

But the warmth and homelike atmosphere of this 56 suite hotel provides convivial surroundings for its special guests. Located in the recently restored Shockoe Slip district of Richmond, this European-style hotel sits adjacent to the state capitol of Virginia and the Governor's mansion.

The owner requested that the character of the hotel be timeless in design with remembrance of an elegant past. The design concept was based on this premise and achieved through the use of special building materials, custom furnishings, extensive cherry millwork design and intimate space design. Many of the locals think the hotel was a renovation of an historic building, thus confirming the original design goal.

ARCHITECTURE
Stauffer Associates
INTERIOR DESIGN
Thomas W. Hamilton / Elissa A. Shoolroy
PHOTOGRAPHY
Maxwell Mackenzie

The elegant homelike atmosphere of this small luxury hotel is created through the extensive use of cherry millwork and custom furnishings.

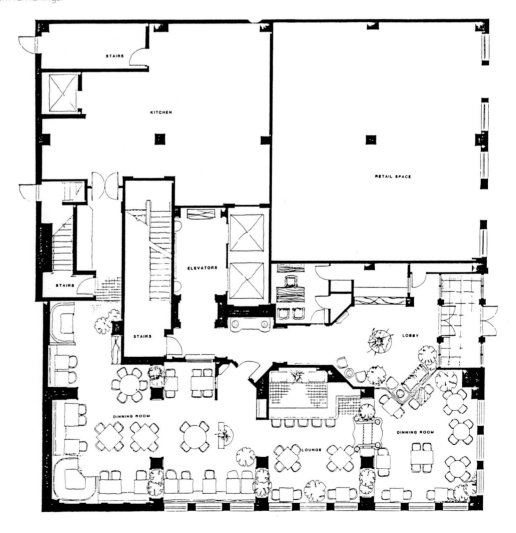

# Bryson Hotel

*MELBOURNE, AUSTRALIA*

To many, a hotel is an exciting and dramatic, albeit short term, experience. Much the same could be said of theater. Therefore, when the new owners of the Bryson Hotel were looking for a design theme, entertainment and theater were the answers. It didn't hurt that the property happened to be situated in the heart of Melbourne's theater and entertainment district.

The theatrical theme becomes most evident in the restaurant and lounge, even set designers were engaged to design the interiors in order to give them variety of movement and depth. An eclectic array of building facades enclose the individual bars and form a backdrop to the dance floor, creating an atmosphere where revelers can escape into a make believe world of yesteryear Hollywood.

Movie memorabilia adorn the individually themed areas of the theater restaurant.

The entertainment areas of the hotel are much more attuned to the theme, leaving a more subtle homelike atmosphere in the lobby and guestrooms. The lobby dons a circular coffered ceiling highlighted by recessed lighting. False columns were introduced to promote the symmetry of the central vista. The use of natural timber paneling complimented by rich parquet flooring and hand-made Tai-Ping carpet inlays create a feeling of warmth. Carefully chosen European and Oriental antique pieces provide artistic focal points.

HOTEL COMPANY
Rydges Hotel Group
INTERIOR DESIGN
Pacific Design Group
PHOTOGRAPHY
Otto Rogge

# Chateau Whistler Resort

*WHISTLER, BRITISH COLUMBIA, CANADA*

**A**lthough it had been almost a century since one of the Canadian Pacific chateau properties had been constructed, this beautiful country house hotel, the Chateau Whistler, features turn-of-the-century chateau designs including dancing roof lines, gargoyles and rustic fortress bases.

**S**pace planning echoed features of other chateau properties. The "Great Hall" becomes the chateau lobby signaling grand vertical, awe-inspiring spaces. Chateau Whistler's 40 foot peaked ceiling is supported by rustic 5 foot square columns of squamish rock. The lobby is paved in green slate set in a geometric pattern, reminiscent of those seen on European chateau terraces. Adding accent to the slate flooring are several Mennonite-inspired hooked rugs. Accent slate colors of ocher, terracotta and red signal the way to guest services such as the front desk, the elevator lobby and the grand staircase.

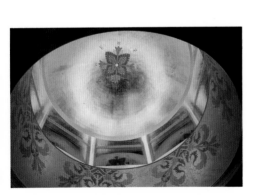

The Great Hall echoes chateau lobbies featuring a grand ceiling of 40 feet with five foot square columns of squamish rock.

This imposing chateau features the best of country house design with the modern conveniences of current construction.

Almost every setting of the baronial hotel features local artifact and antiques representative of early Canada. Young artists and native sculptors were commissioned from British Columbia for special art pieces. Even the casual guestroom decor features antique blanket boxes and country art.

HOTEL COMPANY
Canadian Pacific Hotels and Resorts
ARCHITECTURE
Pnenburg/Tibbatts Design Inc

# Checkers Hotel Kempinski

*LOS ANGELES, CALIFORNIA, USA*

The exterior facade features lovingly restored Spanish Baroque plaster details and etched glass deco style doors.

It's not often that a true "gem of a hotel" is created, but the new Checkers Hotel Kempinski in Los Angeles certainly qualifies.

Not only did the owner, William Wilkinson president of Ayala Hotels, assemble an incredible team of talent to produce this structure, but clearly Wilkinson himself had the vision and acute sense of style needed to develop this magnificent project. The challenge was to transform the shell of an historic landmark hotel into the only small luxury hotel located in the heart of downtown Los Angeles.

*The Lobby lounge with Coromandel screen: Chinese incised lacquer decoration on wood.*

Renovation of this 1927 building comprised infinite technicalities connected with modernizing facilities and conforming with building codes. Wilkinson chose Holtsmark and Kaplan/McLaughlin/Diaz as architects to create Checkers from the former Mayflower Hotel. After four years of construction, Holtsmark reflected that..."it's a beautiful jewel reflecting the grand past amidst all the glass boxes and modern buildings in downtown L.A." Non-historic elements were removed, exterior stucco was removed and replaced, and entire floors were replaced in order to reconfigure room dimensions without compromise of structural features. By means of resourceful space planning and the desire for spacious and elegant bedrooms, 346 very small guest rooms were turned into 190 more elegant ones. A new two-story penthouse and rooftop lap pool with a view of the downtown skyline complete the luxurious setting.

The intimate Mezzanine library features plush charcoal velvet sofas with silk pillows, and two 12th Century Sung Dynasty terracotta burial urns.

Interiors were created by the talent of James Northcutt Associates, creators of such elegant interiors as the Mansion on Turtle Creek in Dallas, the Biltmore in Santa Barbara, and the Four Seasons in Newport Beach, California. The interiors have a transitional and eclectic style, a contemporary classicism that blends Art Deco, oriental and contemporary. According to Northcutt, "We have created a hotel of understated and simple elegance. One which evokes an atmosphere of graciousness and comfort. We want our guests to be enriched by their surroundings without being overwhelmed, and we have succeeded in accomplishing our objective."

HOTEL COMPANY
*Kempinski*
ARCHITECTURE
*Holtsmark Architects, Kaplan/McLaughlin/Diaz*
INTERIOR DESIGN
*James Northcutt Associates*
PHOTOGRAPHY
*Jaime Ardiles-Arce*

The living room of 3-Bay Penthouse suite includes many pieces of original artwork such as the Richard Diebenkorn etched prints.

An executive suite features a dining area converted from a former outdoor terrace and original outdoor mouldings.

# Doral Park Avenue Hotel

*New York City, New York, USA*

The recent metamorphosis of this intimate neighborhood hostelry has upgraded its first class designation to a true deluxe hotel. All that is left of the old Doral Park Avenue structure is the canopy, the elevators and the walls. The bones of this neoclassical hotel were built in the 1920s, but the recent renovation has created a modern romantic hotel with early Italian and Greek influences.

A truly imposing feature is the Grand Stair, rising from the lobby to the meeting/private dining rooms above. The black stair of marble and mirror lighted with bronze hand-held candles was inspired by fairy tales of the past. The bronze railing was designed by Ruhlmann in the 1920s for a Parisian department store.

The black stair of marble and mirror features hand-held candles inspired by Jean Cocteau's Beauty and the Beast.

The classic good looks of the bar are indicative of the hotel's neoclassical style.

The limitations of space were the greatest renovation challenge. But the determination to appeal to the discriminating and sophisticated traveler was the needed impetus. The designers searched out fine muralists with classical talents and painstakingly designed doorways, walls, windows, stairways; the tedious rearrangement of spaces was like a massive jigsaw puzzle.

Every inch of this special hotel has been considered for the comfort and aesthetic senses of its appreciative guests.

HOTEL COMPANY
Doral Hotels & Resorts
INTERIOR DESIGN
Tom Lee Limited
PHOTOGRAPHY
Jaime Ardiles-Arce

# Embassy Suites Times Square

*NEW YORK, NEW YORK, USA*

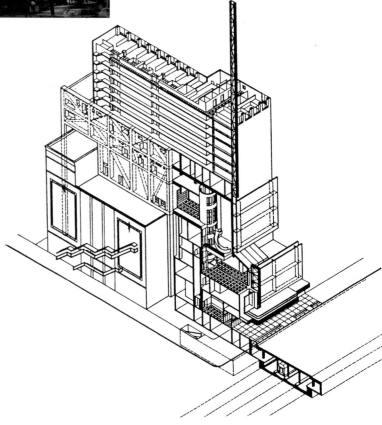

It's unusual, but not unheard of, to convert an old building into a hotel, but it is indeed rare to build a hotel around an existing edifice. But that is precisely what happened when the new Embassy Suites Times Square was built around the 75-year-old landmark Palace Theater. "By embracing the unique elements of this site, the building is one where form is integrated with culture," explains Bruce Fowle.

The vibrantly colored glass and masonry hotel, which includes six levels of interior public spaces, rises 43 stories over and adjacent to the existing Palace Theater, once the premier showcase for vaudeville and one of New York's foremost Broadway theaters. Concrete-encased steel trusses span the theater. The design includes a new marquee and a series of lobbies which make the transition from the building's contemporary exterior to the traditional character of the existing hall. The facade of the hotel tower is blue-tinted glass with two shades of gray clay-coated brick and red and blue glazed brick accents. The design won a *Progressive Architecture* magazine award in 1989.

HOTEL COMPANY
Embassy Suites
**ARCHITECTURE**
Fox & Fowle Architects, P.C.
**INTERIOR DESIGN**
Fox & Fowle Interiors
**PHOTOGRAPHY**
Peter Paige, Interior
Andrew Gordon, Exterior

WEST 47TH STREET

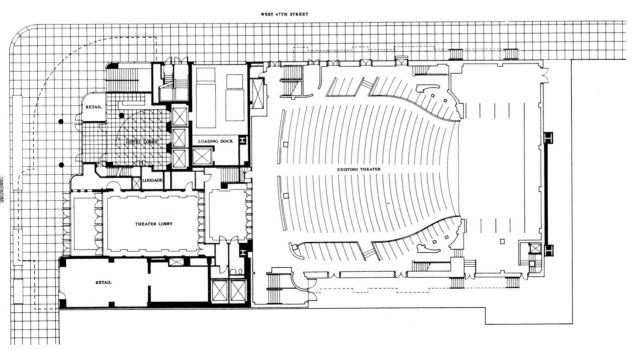

RETAIL

HOTEL LOBBY      LOADING DOCK

LUGGAGE

EXISTING THEATER

THEATER LOBBY

RETAIL

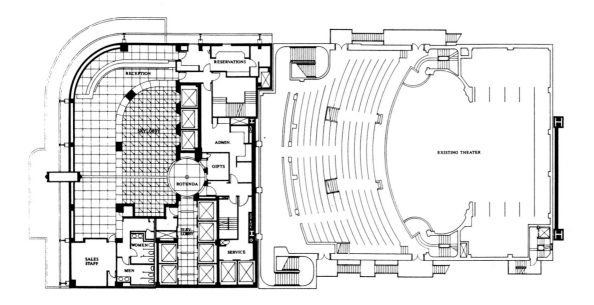

The contemporary design of the interiors brings in elements of post modern design with a twist of theater accents.

# Empress Hotel

*VICTORIA, CANADA*

The opulent elegance of an era now past has been restored to the venerable Empress Hotel, the legendary destination resort in Victoria. The Canadian Pacific Hotel has not only undergone a complete refurbishment, but it is now linked to the recently constructed Victoria Conference Center on one side and its own newly constructed guest registration pavilion, elevator tower and health club and pool on the other.

The design team, Deborah Lloyd Forrest Associates, interior designers of Dallas, and Poon-Carruthers Architects, researched old drawings and photographs to restore the hotel to its original splendor. An immense amount of time was invested in studying Victorian and Edwardian interiors, colors and intensities of colors appropriate to the opening in 1908. The interiors follow the classical yet lush design dictates of the English colonial Victorian design.

The grandness of the period begins in the newly redesigned lobby area. Its ceilings are more than five meters high, supporting twelve original chandeliers. The elegant hardwood floors made of rift-cut white oak, walnut and exotic Brazilian red bean wood had been hidden under wall-to-wall carpet for more than 30 years. Also existing and restored were 16 original bronze ram's head wall sconces and two pair of large bronze andirons with crowns, lions paw bases and ionic columns.

In The Palm Court, the designers uncovered one of the hotel's greatest hidden treasures when an acoustical ceiling and fluorescent fixtures were removed to reveal an enormous dome which was originally the hotel's centerpiece. A new, historically appropriate stained glass pattern was designed and built to fit the original dome structure.

Throughout the property, various original designs and accessories were restored. In the Crystal Ballroom, the original crystal beaded ball chandeliers sporting bronze crowns were removed, cleaned and all 8,000 beads on each re-strung and carefully reinstalled. In the hotel's formal dining room several strong architectural elements were restored including tudor arches, columns with elaborate plaster corbelled brackets supporting carved wood beams, leaded glass upper window panels with stained glass medallion centers, and a massive chateau-style woodburning fireplace.

HOTEL COMPANY
Canadian Pacific Hotels & Resorts
ARCHITECTURE
Poon-Carruthers Architects
INTERIOR DESIGN
Deborah Lloyd Forrest Associates

The deluxe guestrooms feature such special touches as decorative fireplaces, turret spaces, elegant armoires and carefully selected accents and artwork.

Wall-to-wall carpeting was removed
from the lobby to reveal the original
hardwood floors.

# Hotel Excelsior Roma

*ROME, ITALY*

**T**he neoclassical style of this venerable Roman hotel was chosen because of the inventory of authentic pieces of neoclassical furniture which were owned by Ciga Hotels. Many of these fabulous pieces of furniture art now reside in some rooms and corridors of this classic beauty.

The neoclassical style of this hall is a
perfect example of the detail applied to
the restoration of the Hotel Excelsior Roma.

A comfortable yet stylish bedroom of
the hotel.

During the three-year restoration, an intense commitment to neoclassical style was pervasive. Luigi Filippo furniture was added to Ciga's collection as well as having architectural bronze pieces restored according to the original design of that period. Throughout the hotel, antique gold decorations were added as 1800s style dicatates.

Of the hotel's 400 guestrooms, 170 have been completely renovated and a royal suite has been added to the palatial grounds of this classic hotel.

HOTEL COMPANY
Ciga Hotels
**INTERIOR DESIGN**
Mauro Beneditti

# Four Seasons Hotel

*CHICAGO, ILLINOIS, USA*

Rich tapestries and cozy seating areas provide the ideal setting for afternoon tea in the lobby lounge.

World-class luxury abounds at the Four Seasons Chicago. This mixed-use property opened in 1989 on this prime property on North Michigan Avenue. Touted as an innovative, highly-acclaimed, multi-use complex of prime retail, residential and office space, this property combines most of the components of urban living under one roof.

The Conservatory, designed in rich English furnishings and details.

The elegantly appointed lobby of the
Four Seasons Chicago rests on the
seventh floor of a multi-use complex.

Hotel guests enter on the street level and are ushered by elevator to the reception, dining, lounge and meeting room areas on the seventh floor. The feeling one has when entering this hotel is that of a fine and elegant residence. The interiors are appointed with richly upholstered English furnishings, custom-woven carpets and tapestries and hand-crafted armoires.

Although this hotel sits high above the windy city, patrons feel the warmth and elegance of a private estate.

HOTEL COMPANY
*Four Seasons Hotels*
ARCHITECT
*Kohn Peterson Fox and Perkins & Wills*
INTERIOR DESIGN
*Frank Nicholson Incorporated*
PHOTOGRAPHY
*Jaime Ardiles-Arce*

# Four Seasons Resort Wailea

*WAILEA, MAUI, HAWAII*

**W**hen the owner envisioned the project, he made it very clear to the architects: he wanted to have a "palace" in Hawaii—a 300 to 400 room resort hotel, grand in style and scale. Thus, the Four Seasons Resort Wailea was born.

**T**he concept of palace was developed, in part with the symmetry and formal pattern of the building, its grand staircase, courts, gardens, pools and fountains. The basic colonnade theme was chosen for its classical, palatial character complimented by large tile overhangs which evoke the feeling of shelter characteristic of much Hawaiian architecture. The concept of outdoor living, by both day and night, is not possible in too many places. However, Hawaii's climate dictates space design that incorporates an abundance of natural light, cross ventilation and the unification of indoor and outdoor spaces.

Both dining and other public areas of the hotel are partially open to the elements to provide a feeling of continuous outdoor living.

Most of the furnishings in this palatial resort feature oversized, comfortable seatings with casual fabrics and natural art accents.

Considerable public space that would ordinarily be perceived as rooms are partially open, richly appointed verandas flowing casually from one area to another. Even hallways in guestroom wings atypically have natural light and ventilation, no air-conditioning, just year-round prevailing winds to provide circulation.

Thus, the grandeur of the project's distinctly palatial character is combined with openness and informal flow of spaces, breezes that are invited in, shade amply provided where needed, a light color palette, and a generous use of tropical greenery and exotic flowers ensure that this resort functions as tropical architecture.

**HOTEL COMPANY**
*Four Seasons Resort*
**ARCHITECTURE**
*Wimberly Allison Tong & Goo*
**INTERIOR DESIGN**
*James Northcutt Associates*
**PHOTOGRAPHY**
*Jaime Ardiles-Arce*

# Grand Floridian Beach Resort

*WALT DISNEY WORLD, FLORIDA*

When the hotel's owner starts talking about creating a fantasy destination and wants to bring in his "imagineering" people to help create the hotel's "backstage" and staff "costumes", you know you're not dealing with just any hotel property. But then again, working with Disney Development Company is not like any other company.

After toying with a number of Asian themes for the resort, Disney eventually settled on a turn of the century grand classic Victorian-style hotel designed to mirror a combination of the Grand Hotel on Mackinac Island, The Del Coronado near San Diego and the Bellevue Biltmore in nearby Clearwater. And when Disney does it, they do it right. The resort rings true both in its details and its overall design. The buildings may be a bit theatrical, but they are not just stage sets. Distinctive towers, striking red shingle roofs, dormers, cupolas, exposed gable trusses and pristine white clapboard exteriors recall the Victorian era. Gables feature decorative white painted cedar shingles in a variety of designs.

The grand Victorian architecture features cupolas, red roof shingles, dormers, exposed gable trusses and white clapboard exteriors.

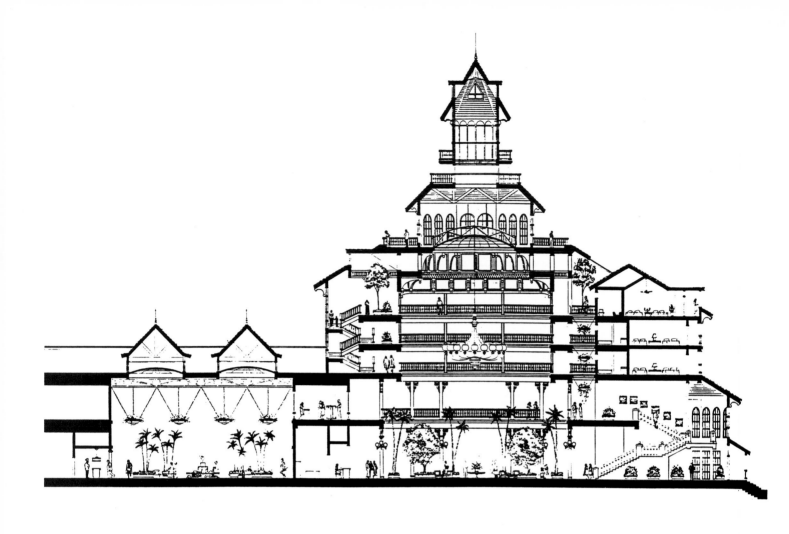

The magnificent five-story atrium Grand Lobby has a ceiling adorned with three illuminated stained-glass domes and hanging chandeliers.

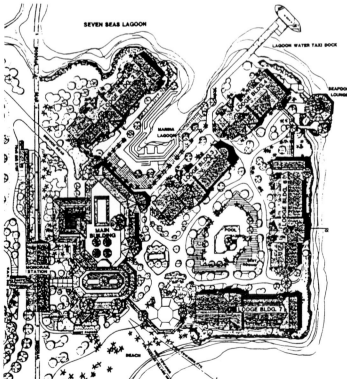

The Victorian theme has, naturally, been carried throughout the project. Ceiling fans, gas lamps, intricate lattice work, wide verandas and an abundant use of wicker emphasize the Victorian seaside hotel ambience. There are even attic guestrooms built into the dormers of the roof structure which have become the most popular rooms in the hotel.

HOTEL COMPANY
*Disney Development Company*
ARCHITECTURE
*Wimberly Allison Tong & Goo*
INTERIOR DESIGN
*Wimberly Allison Tong & Goo*
PHOTOGRAPHY
*Berger/Conser — Ronald Moore & Associates*

# Grand Hotel Firenze

*FLORENCE, ITALY*

The fabulous Sala Delle Feste features
gilded antique furnishings, a frescoed
caisson ceiling and authentic Tuscan
Renaissance architecture.

**A**fter almost two and one half years of
painstaking restoration, the Grand Hotel
Firenze has been completely refurbished
in splendid Tuscan Renaissance style.
This Five Star jewel in the Ciga Hotels
crown sits majestically in the heart of
downtown Florence, the birthplace of the
Renaissance and the center of style for
the old world.

The refurbishment encompassed the entire hotel, but focused particularly on the main function rooms and the guestrooms. These newly-created rooms feature magnificent frescoes copied from churches and convents, caisson ceilings copied from Palazzo Davanzati, antique furniture and furniture inspired by original designs. The result is an historical work of art. For the true Renaissance afficionado, this is the place to stay in Tuscany.

HOTEL COMPANY
Ciga Hotels
**ARCHITECTURE**
Papiri Collection

One of the new guestrooms of the hotel features classic Tuscan Renaissance design featuring a frescoed wall depicting typical Tuscan lifestyle from long ago.

# Grand Hyatt Hong Kong

*HONG KONG*

**F**or many years, Hong Kong has combined the cosmopolitan western world with the mysterious Orient. Grand Hyatt continues this theme but adds the elegance of the past with the sophistication of today. Fronting one of the most picturesque harbors in the world, Grand Hyatt Hong Kong goes beyond the image of a modern hotel and redefines luxury with classical standards of excellence. Deservedly, it is Hyatt International's flagship hotel.

**R**eminiscent of the grand old European hotels at the turn of the century, the 573-room, five star hotel has been an award winner in almost every category of hotelkeeping  The exterior architecture features the boldness of polished marble and the strength of silvered glass creating a truly futuristic design for a hotel. But as imposing as the exterior is, the warmth and tradition of the interior creates a comfortable yet elegant haven for international travelers.

The dramatic use of marble and curvaceous architectural lines create a lobby environment reminiscent of elegant oceanliners of the past.

The interiors of the Grand Hyatt Hong Kong are best described as a return to the elegance in the 1930s with its focus on luxury, high society and Art Deco designs. The bold colors and graphic representations are evident in the lobby which almost resembles the salon of an ocean-going passenger liner of that era. With one of the most magnificent views of the harbor, the lobby is tastefully furnished with period pieces, marbled columns and graceful statuettes. Other dramatic public areas of the hotel feature marble and granite from Italy and Spain, natural foliage and water features.

Just as striking as the design is the luxury of space. Even the opulent bathrooms, featuring an abundance of marble and mirror, are meant to be lived in and enjoyed, all the luxuries of a well-appointed bath are here.

According to the hotel's general manager Peter Jentes, "The Grand Hyatt is a bridge with the romantic past and a link with the exciting future."

HOTEL COMPANY
Hyatt International Corporation

The elegant marble and mirror bathrooms feature gold fixtures and all the amenities of a well-appointed home.

An elegant suite at the Grand Hyatt provides the most elegant of features with arguably the most magnificent view of Hong Kong harbor.

# The Harbor View Hotel

*MARTHA'S VINEYARD, MASSACHUSETTS, USA*

Although the hotel was completely gutted, the new architecture and details including crown moldings, door designs and light fixtures are taken straight from designs of Victorian seaside summer resorts.

In the late-1800s, when Edgartown, Massachusetts was a thriving whaling port, a new summer hotel was commissioned on the edge of the island. Built in the Victorian manner, the Harbor View Hotel quicky became the active hub of this community on Martha's Vineyard. Because of the hotel's success, in 1910, a wing of an abandoned hotel on another part of the island was moved across the island and added to the hotel.

Though the Hotel served a century of summer vacationers, when new owners purchased the property in 1989, the entire hotel needed rebuilding. Using photographs from Victorian seacoast resorts, the property was gutted and totally remodeled. The new year-round Harbor View Hotel has been the recipient of numerous awards including the 1991 ASID winner of the best renovation in the historic preservation category and the 1991 Interior Design Awards by *Restaurants & Institutions Magazine*.

The lobby is decorated in weathered
earth tones and sunwashed shades of
a typical Victorian summer resort.

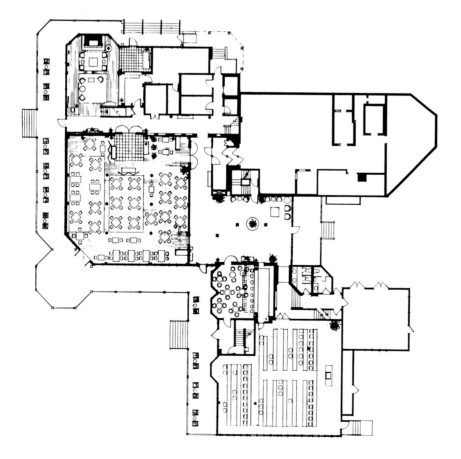

**A**ll that remains of the old hotel is the
original natural stone fireplace in the
lobby. New ceiling moldings and other
architectural details reminiscent of turn-of-
the-century Victorian style were added for
richness and character. The interiors feature wicker lounge chairs upholstered in
opulent floral tapestry in weathered earth
tones and sunwashed shades of egg-
shell, cream, and sandstone combined
with deeper tones of green.

**O**f the 129 bedrooms, the 88 new guestrooms feature turn-of-the-century romantic
interiors including old-fashioned iron
beds, dark green wicker furniture, simple
striped linen draperies, ecru eyelet sheers,
custom pecan-washed armoires, period
iron lamps and aged patina wallcoverings.

HOTEL COMPANY
Winthrop Hotels & Resorts
ARCHITECTURE
The Preservation Partnership
INTERIOR DESIGN
FORMA
PHOTOGRAPHY
Robert Miller, Jack Weinhold

# Hyatt Fisherman's Wharf

*SAN FRANCISCO, CALIFORNIA, USA*

The main lobby features a cozy spot by the fireplace for warm relaxation after a day on the Wharf.

Massive features of French limestone
were installed in the public areas such
as this entry staircase at Taylor Street.

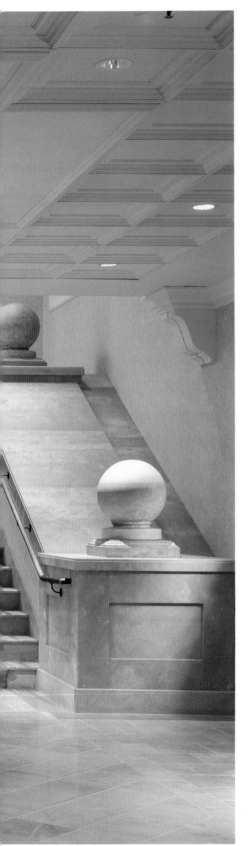

The San Francisco earthquake of 1906 created mass destruction, but from its rubble in 1907 was born the masonry-constructed warehouse of the Musto Marble Works. Although the building was not architecturally significant for its time, the old warehouse has given style and architectural importance to the new Hyatt Fisherman's Wharf housed in its halls.

While most of the other hotels near this famous landmark feature more of a "by the sea" theme, the Hyatt has clung to its grander Victorian roots. The building's history is strongly expressed in the restaurant, housed in the main volume of the original warehouse. Original brick walls and redwood timbers are exposed, giving texture and character to this Italian-style bistro. The old finishes are playfully enriched with brightly hued ceramic and marble tiles, bold splashes of wall color and copper.

Throughout the rest of the hotel, the Victorian reference is more elegant and understated. The lobby features touches of cast terra cotta panels and a resplendent wood burning fireplace to warm tourists.

The furnishings at this Hyatt remain approachable and comfortable. French limestone, distressed woods, rich carpets, tables which invite tired feet to rest, wicker safari chairs and sofas deep enough to disappear in, welcome families and business travelers alike.

HOTEL COMPANY
Hyatt Corporation
ARCHITECTURE
Hill Architects
INTERIOR DESIGN
Blair Spangler
PHOTOGRAPHY
Chas McGrath

# Hyatt Hotel

*CHARLOTTE, NORTH CAROLINA, USA*

The lobby area resembles an Italian courtyard with its cantera stone floors and pavers.

The challenge in this design was to create the first down-scaled prototype for Hyatt while still maintaining the sense of luxury which has become synonymous with the Hyatt image. The designers took the Hyatt atrium concept one step further by providing the weary traveler with a casual outdoor piazza designed to emanate from the lobby area. The Old-World feeling of the Colorado quartz stone floor and adoquin stone fountain create a soothing escape for the weary business traveler. Throughout the atrium, intricate ironwork railing details echo the Italianate atmosphere.

This 267-room project includes a six-story main building and a four-story atrium. This 21 month interior design project was the winner of the 1990 Gold Key Award from the American Hotel & Motel Association for the most outstanding lobby area in a hotel.

**HOTEL COMPANY**
Hyatt Hotels Corporation
**INTERIOR DESIGN**
INDEX The Design Firm
**PHOTOGRAPHY**
Creative Resources Photography / Rion Rizzo

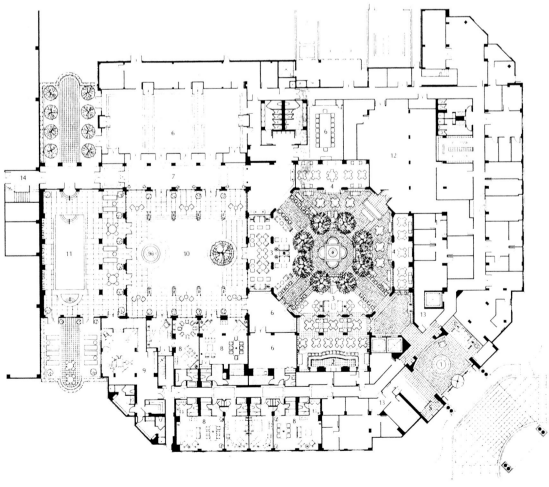

The casual restaurant atmosphere includes stone floors and Italian wicker cafe chairs that impart a light airy feeling.

# Hyatt on Collins

*MELBOURNE, VICTORIA, AUSTRALIA*

Listed as the recipient of the 1990 Australian Tourism Award's most luxurious hotel, this elegant addition to Melbourne's prestigious Collins Street is itself an historic site.

As Australia celebrates its bicentennial, the two hundredth anniversary of European settlement here, this new hotel celebrates Australia's unique national identity. The owner, Max Moar, took an unusual approach to building this elegant Hyatt; he insisted on the best of everything—an unusual request in Australia where limited resources require most luxury items to be imported.

The reception area features extensive use of Italian marble and an original acrylic painting by Australian artist Paul Partos.

The luxurious marble bathrooms display the spare-no-expense philosophy of the hotel's owner.

The scale of this luxurious hotel is appropriate to Melbourne's proud heritage of Victorian hospitality. In the 19th Century, that tradition was translated architecturally through a tendency to emphasize the individual by avoiding awesomely spacious volumes. Therefore, most of the ceilings in this hotel soar at a much lower level than the atria in many other Hyatts.

Featuring, among other details, 25,000 square meters of Italian marble, this hotel glistens within a multi-faceted, gold-glazed tower. The overall style is sleekly contemporary and fashionably Art Deco with a strong emphasis on an outstanding collection of fine art.

HOTEL COMPANY
Hyatt International Corporation
ARCHITECTURE
Peddle, Thorp & Learmonth
INTERIOR DESIGN
Hirsch-Bedner & Associates
PHOTOGRAPHY
Jaime Ardiles-Arce

# Hyatt Regency

*Kauai, Hawaii, USA*

The future of Hawaii lies in its past. Such was the design philosophy of the new Hyatt Regency Kauai—a Hawaiian hotel that actually feels like a Hawaiian hotel. This $200 million hotel is all new, but it feels comfortable and somehow familiar.

On 50 oceanfront acres, the 600-room Hyatt Regency Kauai stretches across lush gardens and lagoons in classic Hawaiian architecture reminiscent of the 1920s and 1930s.

While the trend in Hawaii has been toward the mega fantasy resorts, this hotel is an example of the newest renaissance in Hawaiian architecture. The developers consciously avoided, at some perceived risk, the trend toward fantasy resorts in favor of an older Hawaii of the 1920s and 30s, one more reminiscent of the old Halekulani and the old Waiohai. Guests will notice the numerous fine touches, Hawaiian artifacts and new Hawaiian crafts that grace the public areas. The three-story oceanfront hotel reflects the steep thatch roof of Hawaii's early vernacular, or grass shack architecture. It recalls the timeless style introduced by Dickey, the father of Hawaii's architecture who adapted the California Mission style to Hawaii's tropical climate and designed such features as wide caves, high open windows and double-pitched roofs.

HOTEL COMPANY
Hyatt
ARCHITECTURE
Wimberly Allison Tong & Goo
INTERIOR DESIGN
Hirsch-Bedner & Associates
PHOTOGRAPHY
Milroy/McAleer

The new Hyatt serves as a showcase for the work of local artists and artisans.

# Hyatt Regency Singapore

*SINGAPORE*

The design directive for this hotel was clear: to create a new international feeling and reconfigure the rooms into new elegant suites.

In order to compete with newer luxury hotels in the lucrative Singapore market, the owners knew they had to make some drastic design and renovation decisions. Wilson & Associates was called in to complete their first project in Asia which required extensive research and management of new sources. The consensus was to take the existing 800-key guestroom tower and convert it to 450 suites that would keep the property competitive well into the year 2000.

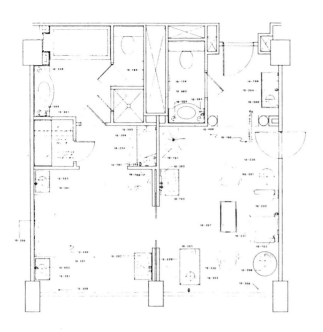

This two-bay guestroom was designed to appeal to the international business traveler's needs for separate working and living areas. The color palette of salmon and celadon is combined with light wood.

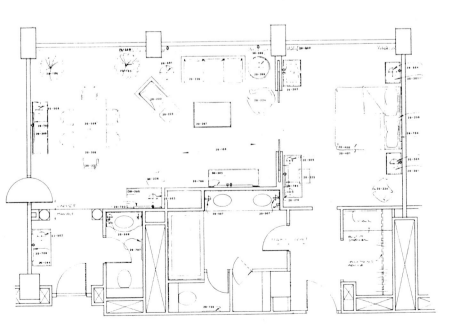

HOTEL COMPANY
Hyatt International
INTERIOR DESIGN
Wilson & Associates'
PHOTOGRAPHY
Jaime Ardiles-Arce

Typical guestroom at the new Hyatt
Regency Singapore.

The extensive use of marble and rich
color accents create livable bathrooms.

# Kingsmill Conference and Sports Center

*WILLIAMSBURG, VIRGINIA, USA*

The rich wood and elegant chair fabrics create a sophisticated yet cozy retreat for business guests.

One of the more recent trends in inn-keeping is to provide the business guest with a variety of experiences during his stay. One way to relax a busy business traveler is to create a casual, yet sophisticated conference environment with the added experience of an on-sight sports and recreation center.

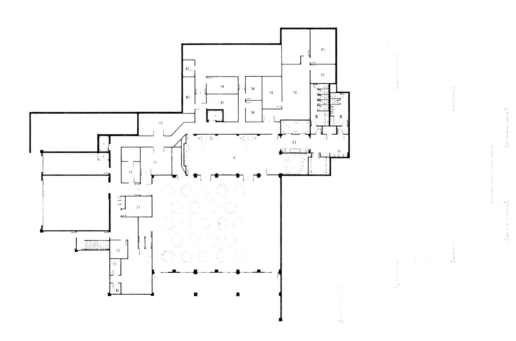

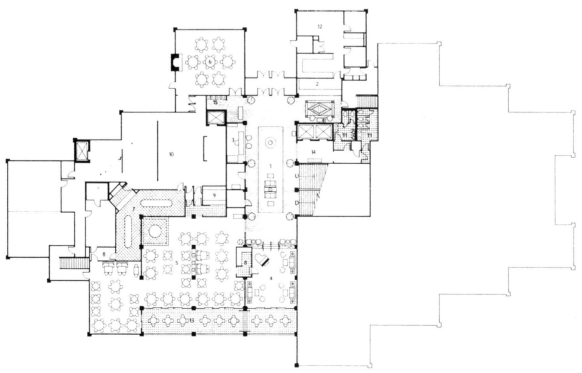

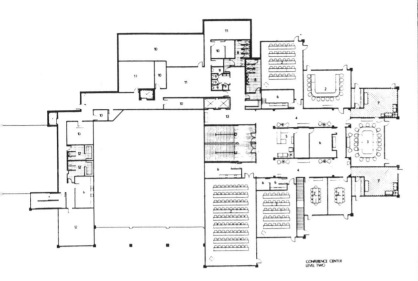

The Kingsmill Conference and Sports Center, located in historic Williamsburg, was required to provide guests with the architectural detailing one would expect in this historic area while still providing a productive business atmosphere and casual relaxing retreat. The furnishings and accessories reflect a combination of colonial and contemporary period-influenced pieces. The stately lobby features imposing 12 foot tall tapering mahogany columns while the conference center is dressed in both Honduras and African mahogany and cherry wood details. The warm feeling in the lounge area is inspired by back-to-back fireplaces and hand-carved tree columns at the bar.

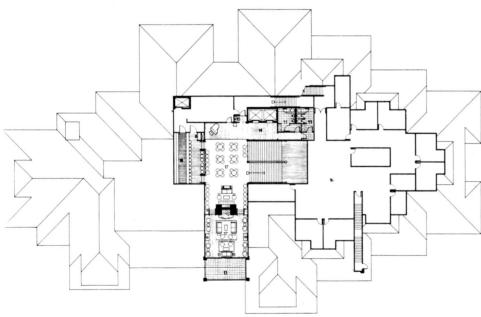

HOTEL COMPANY
Busch Properties
INTERIOR DESIGN
INDEX The Design Firm
PHOTOGRAPHY
Robert Miller Photography

# Kyoto Brighton Hotel

*KYOTO, JAPAN*

**J**ust west of the Kyoto Imperial Palace, in a quiet environment where the elegance of days gone by remains, sits the elegant Kyoto Brighton Hotel. In a city known for its traditional charm and culture, the designers were challenged to build a modern facility, while still retaining the Japanese simplicity indicative of their modern culture.

**T**he project included 183 guest rooms, banquet halls, restaurants, a bar and a charming wedding ceremony hall. And, because the hotel caters mostly to tour- ists, leisurely relaxation was the design theme. One design consideration that was given much deliberation was the use of Juraka color, or harmonious color, which is considered becoming to Kyoto. However, it was necessary to express it in a modern manner. The goal was achieved and a contemporary hotel, steeped in the tradition of the area, is the relaxing result.

INTERIOR DESIGN
Nikken Sekkei Ltd.
PHOTOGRAPHY
SS LTD

The atrium lobby reflects a contemporary, yet comfortable refuge for tourists.

In keeping with tradition, the entrance to the Japanese restaurant is richly wooded with large window expanses, a serene welcome.

# Loews Ventana Canyon Resort

*TUCSON, ARIZONA, USA*

**T**houghts of Tucson usually create images of southwestern or adobe architecture and barren desert. Yet, this is not the image of the Loews Ventana Canyon Resort. Instead, visitors to this enchanting resort are greeted by a more contemporary hotel, reminiscent of Frank Lloyd Wright style. Built of split-faced custom masonry block, this resort hotel was designed to blend into the foothills of the Catalina Mountains. Surrounded by lush desert landscaping and a magnificent natural waterfall, it is anything but barren.

The comfortable Cascade Lounge features dramatic lighting and oversized furnishings.

The four star resort was designed to provide the utmost comfort in this serene setting as a meeting site for weary executives of major corporations. It has become that, but without sacrificing the surrounding desert environment. In fact, this unobtrusive hotel enhances the setting as if it were a sculpture.

The interiors of the 400 room hotel are dressed in casual elegance featuring original art for each guest room and public spaces. While the interior architecture

includes a variety of stone textures and geometric designs, the public spaces showcase oversized furnishing of natural materials and accessories such as huge crystals and fossils. The color palette echoes the natural desert hue.

**HOTEL COMPANY**
Loews
**ARCHITECTURE**
Frizzell Hill Associates, Inc.
**INTERIOR DESIGN**
Hirsch-Bedner & Associates
**PHOTOGRAPHY**
Motoo Okamura, Okamura Design
Shigeru Ohki

# Mansion on Turtle Creek

*DALLAS, TEXAS, USA*

**I**t's hard to find a more elegant spot to enjoy Texas hospitality than the Mansion on Turtle Creek.

**W**hat was once an historic Mediterranean-style mansion now houses one of the most elegant and popular restaurants in Dallas. In the main restaurant, a fireplace at each end and museum-quality art create a grand ambience for the famous southwestern-style food of chef Dean Fearing. In the adjacent bar, the feel is more clubby with dark wood flooring, a low-beamed ceiling, forest green fabric walls and 18th-Century hunting lithographs and paintings.

**T**he entrance foyer to the hotel wing features a 32-foot-high rotunda with arched windows. Recognized as one of the best hotels in the world, each of the unique guestrooms are large, luxuriously comfortable and lavishly appointed. The furnishings are traditional and all art is original.

HOTEL COMPANY
Rosewood Hotels
ARCHITECTURE
Phillip W. Shepherd Architects
INTERIOR DESIGN
Phillip W. Shepherd Architects /
Hirsch-Bedner & Associates

A typical guestroom at the Mansion features large comfortable seating areas and architectural appointments such as cantera stone cornices.

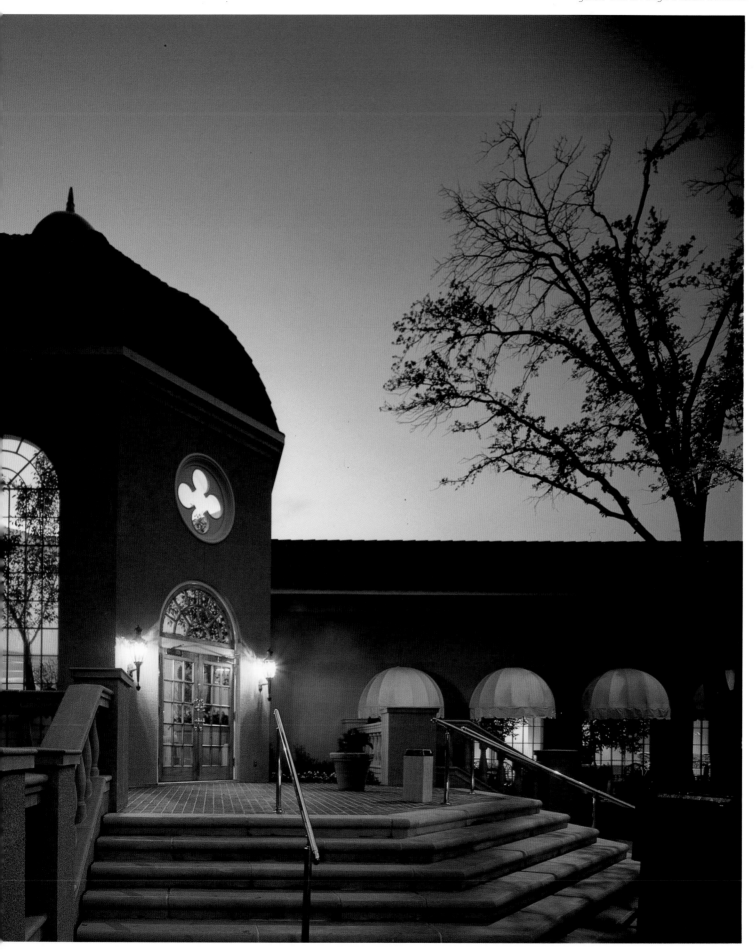

An imposing rotunda, housing the lobby and registration areas, greets guests with an elegant Texas welcome.

# Marriott Suites at Symphony Towers

*SAN DIEGO, CALIFORNIA, USA*

**W**ith its architectural roots deeply embedded in San Diego's 1929 Symphony Hall, the new Marriott Suites at Symphony Towers has a lyrical design quality.

**T**his new 264-suite hotel is part of Symphony Towers, a mixed-use development built atop the restored Symphony Hall. Guests enter the formal lobby at street level where they are greeted with iron and crystal chandeliers in concert with Mexican Marble flooring. The simple barrel vault acknowledges San Diego's mission heritage. Then its 12 floors up to the sky lobby and registration area where the feeling is more of a private courtyard with traditional Spanish architecture. Rich woods and ironwork play against lush foliage. Colors of peach, lemon, melon, orange, kiwi and berry dance across a carpet pattern of florals and lattice work. Mexican marbles and arches encase the lobby lounge while borders of red-flamed granite are a continuation of the rich palette introduced on the building's exterior.

HOTEL COMPANY
Marriott
ARCHITECTURE
Victor Huff Partnership, Inc.
PHOTOGRAPHY
Karl Francetic

Dramatic lighting and rich Mexican marble floors highlight the unique architecture of this former Symphony Hall.

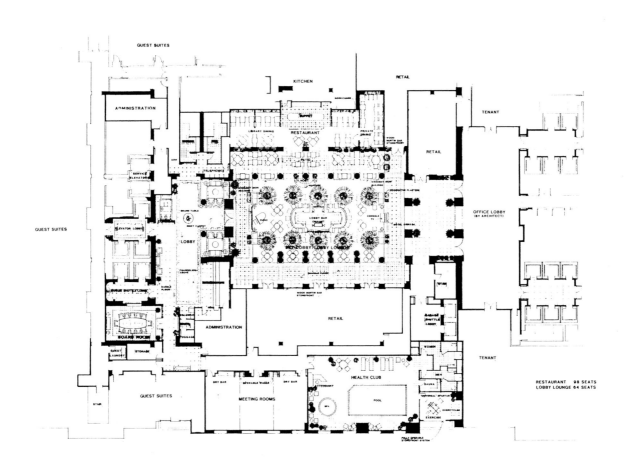

115

Traditional barrel vault ceilings echo San Diego's mission style, and Spanish heritage.

# Mayfair Regent

*Chicago, Illinois, USA*

The old Lake Shore Drive Hotel was a dormant residential hotel until Ellen McCluskey Associates breathed new life into its hallways and created the five star Mayfair Regent Hotel. The project, which took only one year to complete brought back 19th Century elegance which once graced Chicago's Lake Shore Drive.

One of the first challenges in this renovation was to create a reception area complete with modern hotel registration equipment. For this, the designer chose two free-standing antique French desks opposite the cashier's counter. Upon arrival, guests are ushered to the desks and are registered by one of the assistant managers. Service in the grand old style is evident here.

*The lobby lounge was completely renovated to provide guests with a view of Lake Michigan. The classic designs and small seating groups provide an intimate atmosphere for afternoon tea.*

A French theme was chosen for the penthouse breakfast room. The ceiling in the bar area was painted red while the main dining area has a tray ceiling with mirrors to reflect the lake.

**O**ther renovation designs include the lobby lounge which was found to have mirrored arches along the wall, interrupted by hand-painted panels of Chinese wallpaper. The designers saw a clear opportunity to drape the windows to provide a view of Lake Michigan, but the hand-painted murals were then in need of expansion. An artist was hired to make the mural expansion look as if they were original.

HOTEL COMPANY
*Regent International Hotels*
INTERIOR DESIGN
*Ellen McCluskey Associates*
PHOTOGRAPHY
*Peter Paige*

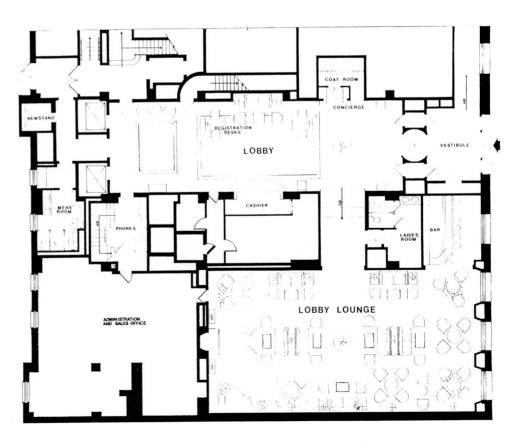

# Nankai South Tower Hotel

*OSAKA, JAPAN*

This stylish hotel was built on top of the Namba Station, a rail terminal, which may eventually have service to the New Kansai Airport. The lobby design was created to function as both a hotel and passenger gathering place in the future.

The rich interiors express an international style with a flavor of the traditional. A strong focus on architectural details such as the grand barrel vaulted ceiling in the French restaurant with stained glass and carved plaster wall accents creates a dramatic room. Lighting and strong use of rich marbles and wood provide striking architectural interest.

INTERIOR DESIGN
Nikken Sekkei Ltd.
PHOTOGRAPHY
Hiroshi Fujiwara

*Dramatic lighting and rich building materials make this bar a congenial meeting spot.*

# The Netherland Plaza Hotel

*Cincinnati, Ohio, USA*

"It is a fantasy experience," says designer Rita St. Clair. "People come to a hotel for an occasional grand experience, and this hotel is the perfect place for that."

The return to its original elegance was the fantasy experience for St. Clair who was responsible for "bringing back" the more gracious life of the Netherland Plaza Hotel, one of the few truly high-style grand old hotels in the United States. This magnificent dedication to the real Art Decoratif style was conceived in the Roaring Twenties by developers who demanded quality in materials, craftsmanship and architecture. Their main inspiration came directly from the Paris Exposition Internationales des Arts Decoratifs et Industriels Modernes of 1925, the true birthplace of Art Deco style. When St. Clair was awarded the restoration project, the grandeur of the Netherland Plaza was there, but it had been hidden through the years under various "contemporary" redecorating procedures.

Rita St. Clair, who orchestrated the renovation, is educated and well-respected in Art Deco design. But her client, the hotel's owner, is also well versed in this historic design style—for the owner is the same as when the hotel opened in the 1930s. And, although the main challenge of this restoration was finding competent craftsmen, some of the contractors were the original suppliers for the hotel in 1929. Another major challenge was in restoring the highly detailed surfaces that are composed of rare or nearly impossible to find materials on a limited budget. Much of these challenges were solved by St. Clair who personally supervised the scagliola techniques applied to pilasters after their many layers of paint had been stripped and other painting and texturing finishes achieved by lacquering, glazing, gold-leafing or other more modern methods.

Although most of the furnishings echo the 18th Century, the lines favor more current tastes as does the color palette which includes more rose, mauve, blue green, dark green and warm beige instead of the more dull tones of taupe and cream that were prevalent during the 1920s.

ARCHITECTURE
Rabun, Hatch & Dendy
INTERIOR DESIGN
Rita St. Clair Associates
PHOTOGRAPHY
Norman McGrath

The Palm Court Restaurant ceilings with their exquisite rococo murals are perfectly dedicated to true Art Deco style.

The Hall of Mirrors resembles its name-
sake in Versailles with original detailing
in the railing. The ceiling is painted
Trompe L'oeil and is filled with plaster
work detailing continued in the ballroom visible through the railing.

# Hotel New Otani Osaka

*OSAKA, JAPAN*

The luxurious New Otani Osaka needed to provide guests with a modern, comfortable setting, but needed to break an important trend that was happening with South East Asian hotels. While it was true that hotels in this area needed a more refined modern image, hotels by non-Japanese designers were creating a standard which lacked authenticity. This hotel was to help create the modern standard.

The main lobby of the New Otani Osaka.

The New Otani Osaka's aim was to create a combined international convention hall with a resort hotel. Interior symbolism was emphasized with a pastel color used as the basic tone for the building; strong colors were used for accents. More emphasis was given to guests' desire for aesthetics than to function and durability.

HOTEL COMPANY
New Otani
INTERIOR DESIGN
Nikken Sekkei Ltd.
PHOTOGRAPHY
Karamatus Minoro

# Norfolk Hotel

*London, England*

The Brasserie de la Paix is a traditional French restaurant which reflects French Empire style without being slavish to the style. The chairs feature traditional swan neck arms and the illusion of open air is created by a large metal pergola with pink canopy. A central marble-topped serving station reinforces the French restaurant style.

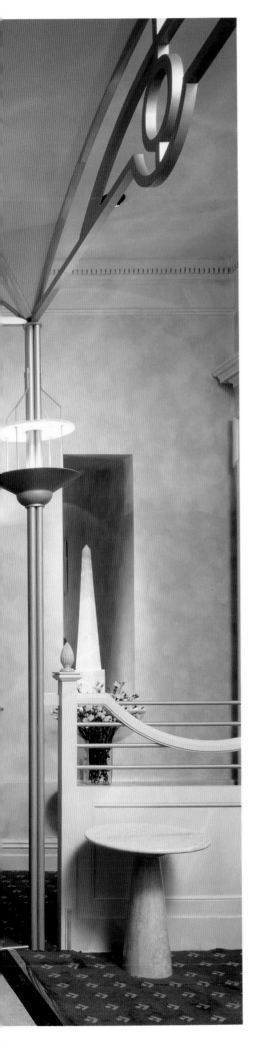

Dry Butlin Bicknell Limited was chosen as architects and interior designers for this unique renovation of a 1870s hotel in South Kensington. DDB recognized that typical modernism was inappropriate for the style of the building and standard of service expected of this four star hotel. Therefore, the designers called for creating warmer, more inviting interiors that inspire a sense of genuine comfort into this special hotel. Inevitably, this has involved a disproportionate amount of effort to refined details and finishes which provide a hotel that is rich and varied in its decor while representing a cohesive entity that is unmistakably unique to the Norfolk.

In order to maximize their investment, DDB suggested that the property contain no less than 100 guest rooms. However, in order to accomplish this task, the roof had to be raised and a new floor added. After lengthy negotiations with the locals and authorities, consent was attained.

Careful attention to detail has been exercised in avoiding the usual rooftop protuberances such as water tanks and mechanical rooms which were re-positioned in lower levels of the hotel.

Interior design features of the Norfolk create a cozy yet interesting combination of styles. Artistic details such as sponging and stippling techniques were applied to the parchment-colored walls complimented by a china blue accent color in the form of balustrades and pilaster capitals. All the metalwork was specially designed, using a hammered finish with brass handrails. The majority of the furnishings were manufactured in Italy including specially-designed mirrors made by a woodcarver in Florence.

HOTEL COMPANY
Norfolk Capital Hotels
ARCHITECTURE
Dry Butlin Bicknell Limited
INTERIOR DESIGN
Dry Butlin Bicknell Limited

# The Phoenician

*SCOTTSDALE, ARIZONA, USA*

**I**n a town known for its fine resorts, Scottsdale's Phoenician resort has soared above the rest. Nestled on 130 acres of rich desert terrain at the base of Camelback Mountain, this 580 room world-class destination resort features elegant accommodations and appointments, fine dining and entertainment, recreation and meeting facilities.

**A**rchitecturally this property is unique. All the buildings are crescent shaped. And, while no two rooms or corridors stack directly above the other, all buildings step back at the fronts and ends. The main structure is almost one quarter mile long. Although expensive, this $260 million resort was mostly built of cast-in-place concrete, designed to last forever and provide maximum energy efficiency.

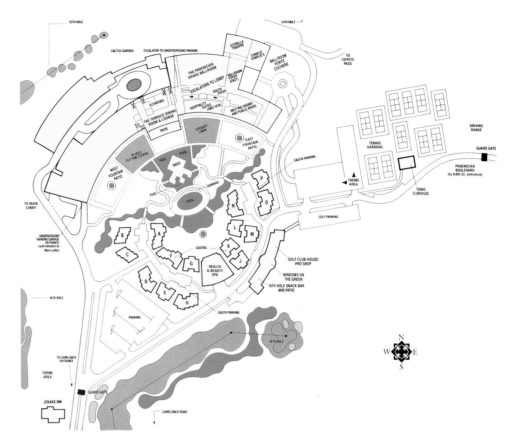

The lobby features an enormous inside fountain and intricate marble flooring.

**B**ecause this property appeals to high-end leisure travelers and high-end corporate meeting and incentive groups, the interiors feature extensive marble and expensive furnishings sprinkled with antiques. The colors are warm desert hues with light-colored accents.

ARCHITECTURE
*Killingsworth, Stricker, Lindgren, Wilson & Associates*

The ballroom foyer provides comfortable yet elegant seating with elegantly paneled walls.

The Windows on the Green Lounge makes a comfortable statement in this desert setting.

# Port de Plaisance

*St. Maarten, Netherland Antilles*

The new Port de Plaisance in St. Maarten is sure to become a famous tropical island getaway. Built mainly for the European market, this development on the Dutch Caribbean island includes 55 acres of tropical beaches, parks, waterfalls, resorts, marina and time share apartments.

The restaurant areas feature light pickled wood, rattan furniture and open walls for cross-ventilation.

A major focus of this French development is an all-suite hotel with interior design by Lynn Wilson Associates. The tropical resort theme is carried throughout the property by open-air spaces. Almost all public spaces are indoor/outdoor with tropical breezes for cross ventilation. The interiors feature light pickled woods, white French limestone floors with turquoise tile insets and flowered fabrics of teal blue and turquoise. All casegoods are natural materials. The all-suite property features art by local Caribbean artists while the public spaces focus on extensive murals. Papier mache tropical fish by Mexican artist Sergio Bustamante adorn the bar area together with other tropical art from Bali.

ARCHITECTURE
Adache Associates
INTERIOR DESIGN
Lynn Wilson Associates
PHOTOGRAPHY
Karl Francetic

# Hotel Quinta Real Guadalajara

*GUADALAJARA, JALISCO, MEXICO*

**A**mid the hustle in the vibrant city of Guadalajara lies an intimate and charming little hotel known as the Hotel Quinta Real. This 50-suite hotel sits like an architectural sculpture in a residential part of this sprawling city. Built mainly from local cantera stone remnants, this charming hotel incorporates all the luxuries of a contemporary five star hotel while preserving the best of Mexican architecture.

145

What guests notice immediately is the comfortable style and strong sense of architectural integrity. According to Elias + Elias, architects, the idea was "to rescue our regional architectural values and show both locals and foreigners that our roots are extremely rich." The charming archways, cantera stone moldings and intricate ironwork show off Mexican handwork at its best.

The lobby is decorated with comfortable seating and Mexican antiques.

**H**andmade details and a plethora of antiques provide an Old World feeling to this hotel. Interior walls are hand sculpted and even the leaded windows in the restaurant appear handmade. Room details include the traditional plaster concha shell headboard and hand forged bathroom fixtures. The public areas are filled with antiques and comfortable oversized furnishings.

ARCHITECTURE
Elias + Elias
PHOTOGRAPHY
Alejandro Lopez

A view into the internal courtyard.

147

The traditional Mexican plaster concha shell is incorporated into the headboard of this suite.

# The Radisson Empire Hotel

*New York City, New York, USA*

The lobby of The Empire creates a castle-like atmosphere for the hotel.

The fine arts of New York's Lincoln Center were the inspiration for the interiors of this hotel built in 1924. Opera is represented in six shadow boxes which are settings of famous operas by the set designer Christian Thee. Lawrence Olivier, painted by a great Washington portrait artist, Brad Stevens, hangs over a marble fireplace and Enrico Caruso and Ellen Terry flank the elevators. The entry of the ballroom is the stage set of Swan Lake represented in three murals inspired by Degas and one of the meeting rooms was designated as the Jazz Room complete with portraits of 18 jazz greats.

*The fine arts of the adjacent Lincoln Center were the inspiration for this hotel's interior design.*

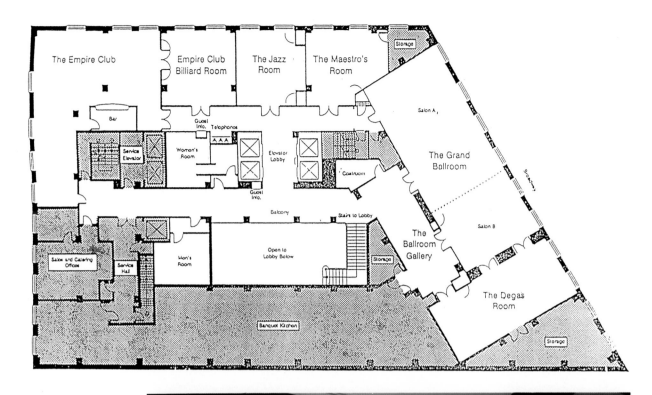

The renovation brings back the Upper West Side hotel's original 1920s charm and classic elegance while adding contemporary amenities for a modern generation of hotel guests. The interior design style is certainly eclectic but focused room by room. The empire room is Old-World style with mahogany paneling, overstuffed green leather chairs and chess and backgammon boards. The lobby has a castle-like atmosphere while the classic lines of the ballroom and its entry are decidedly Roman.

HOTEL COMPANY
Radisson
INTERIOR DESIGN
Tom Lee Limited
PHOTOGRAPHY
Peter Paige

# Radisson Palm Springs Resort And Hotel

*PALM SPRINGS, CALIFORNIA, USA*

The lobby lounge has a comfortable residential feel with the large flagstone fireplace and cozy furniture.

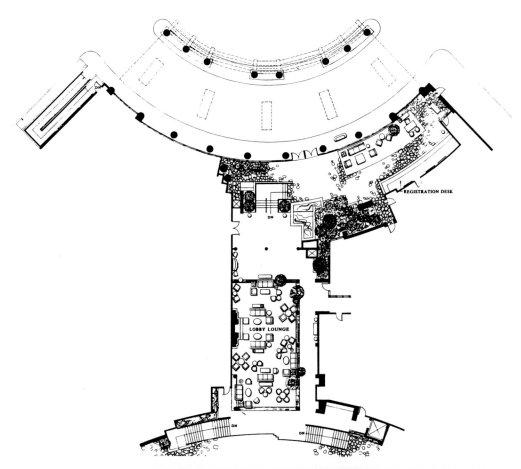

The remodeled lobby greets guests to this California oasis with a lush tropical setting.

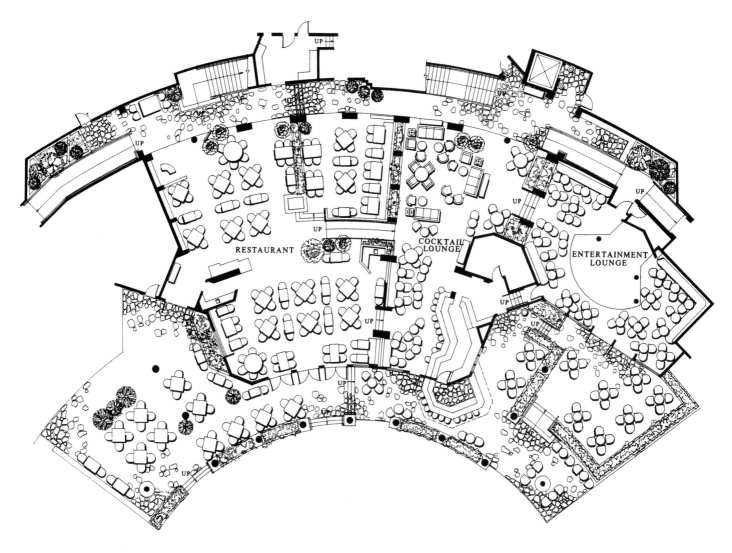

RESTAURANT

COCKTAIL
LOUNGE

ENTERTAINMENT
LOUNGE

The goal was simply defined—to reincarnate a 1950s-style Radisson into a contemporary resort with a decidedly California feel and a timeless look, on a relatively moderate budget and without shutting down the resort.

The goal was achieved and Palm Springs' largest resort hotel is again part of the local vernacular. The newly renovated lobby now looks like a California desert oasis featuring bright open spaces coupled with the casual furnishings, lush plantings and splashing water fountain. The basic color scheme of taupe and beige enlarges the rooms while splashes of turquoise adds brilliant accent. The upper lobby level is now a lobby lounge featuring a large flagstone fireplace with overstuffed furniture, black stained rattan and residential-style tables. Skylights accentuate architectural details in the space and create an outdoor feel.

**HOTEL COMPANY**
Radisson
**ARCHITECTURE**
Arechaederra / Hong / Treiman / Architects
**INTERIOR DESIGN**
Cole Martinez Curtis & Associates
**PHOTOGRAPHY**
Jaime Ardiles-Arce

# Ramada Resort Hotel

*BELDIBI ANTALYA, TURKEY*

Located in the beautiful Turkish resort city of Beldivi Antalya, this five star resort hotel is situated between a pine forest and sandy beach.

The South Antalya Development Project was planned during the 1970s and financed by the World Bank to become a tourist destination for Turkey. It has, in fact, become one of the most successful and beautiful resort areas in the country.

The exterior of this Turkish hotel works with the natural surroundings to blend into the mountains.

The primary controversy over the design of this hotel was its exterior color. Chosen for its ability to blend into the surroundings, from a distance, the hotel seems to vanish into the background. The almost-adobe color and its stepped levels appear almost Southwestern in design, but its contemporary blue entrance and elevator accents make this an eclectic edifice that could be almost anywhere.

The lobby features hand-painted ornamental works, marble arches and rattan furniture.

The interiors of this spacious resort complex are more Moroccan in design. The marble archways, the hand-painted ceilings and wool rugs create a cool setting for the large Rausch rattan furniture. The resort features every activity from Turkish baths and discotheque to casino and archery.

ARCHITECTURE
Ertem Ertunga Architecture
and Urban Planning
INTERIOR DESIGN
Robinson Conn Partnership

# The Regent Beverly Wilshire

*BEVERLY HILLS, CALIFORNIA, USA*

With the redesigned Regent Beverly Wilshire, a finely-crafted, grand, European-style hotel now returns the hotel to its legendary status.

"Our challenge was to create a truly grand hotel in the finest European tradition," says Glenn Texiera, principal of Project Associates who completed the renovation of this world-class hotel. The grand lobby is a magnificent creation of lustrous woods and rich imported marble. Bronze and crystal chandeliers combine with specially created lighting effects to illuminate the beige Bottocino marble columns and glistening mahogany furnishings. Two lobby paintings are reproductions of Marco Ricci originals by Verhoven.

The hotel features a regal lounge, cafe and formal dining areas where guests are surrounded by paneled walls, luxurious silk drapery and custom carpets. Finely crafted antiques, carved tables and chairs and deep sofas add comfort.

*The lobby and lounge feature golden honey-colored paneled walls with silk draperies and rich tables and chairs.*

INTERIOR DESIGN
Project Associates

164

# The Ritz-Carlton

*NAPLES, FLORIDA, USA*

The palatial Ritz-Carlton Naples exudes an air of tradition that belies its recent construction. This new hotel recalls the classic formality of earlier grand old resorts. Its Mediterranean theme establishes a commanding sense of place with symmetry, arches and arcades, bell towers, gardens, fountains and pools. Appropriate to the Florida climate, windows are under protective arcades or shaded by balconies, creating an articulated facade for sun control. Guest rooms overlook a terraced, landscaped court which leads to a lagoon bordering the beach area. Each guestroom has a view of the Gulf.

Interiors are decidedly European, featuring rich silk and brocade fabrics, lush carpets and deep wood accents. Antiques are placed elegantly throughout the hotel.

HOTEL COMPANY
Ritz-Carlton
**ARCHITECTURE**
Wimberly Allison Tong & Goo / Milton Pate
**PHOTOGRAPHY**
Milroy / McAleer

The palatial architecture of the hotel recalls a classic formality.

The elegant European air of the lobby
establishes the interior theme of the
hotel.

# The Ritz-Carlton

*Rancho Mirage, California, USA*

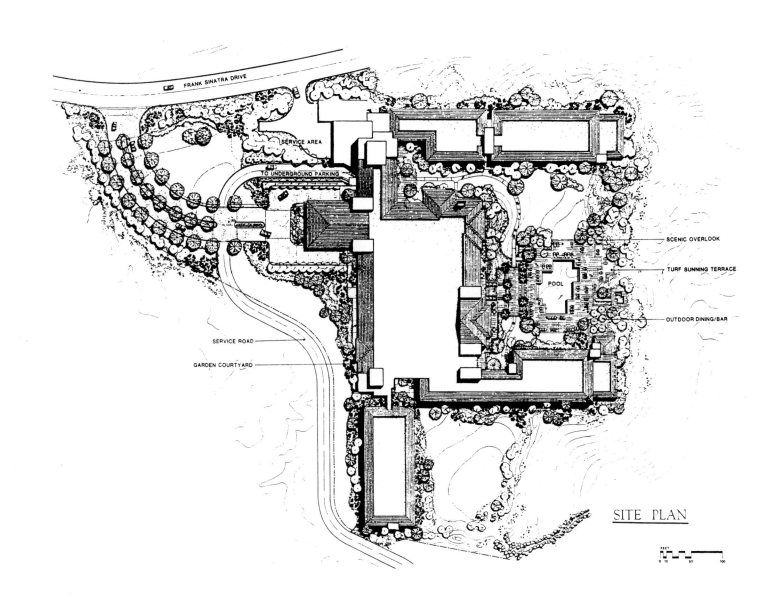

FRANK SINATRA DRIVE

SERVICE AREA

TO UNDERGROUND PARKING

SCENIC OVERLOOK

TURF SUNNING TERRACE

POOL

OUTDOOR DINING/BAR

SERVICE ROAD

GARDEN COURTYARD

SITE PLAN

FEET
0  10        50        100

The Ritz-Carlton in Rancho Mirage is a luxury resort in the middle of an exclusive residential development called The Mirada. The only hillside retreat in the Palm Springs area, the hotel is perched on a wide plateau near the base of the Santa Rosa Mountains and affords a panoramic view of the desert, the valley and distant mountain ranges.

The hotel was designed to blend with the desert environment while providing an exclusive oasis for guests. ''We chose an architectural vocabulary responsive to the climate and setting,'' says Ronald O. Van Pelt senior project designer for the architects. ''Sun Control was a major consideration.'' Stone walls and stately palms lead to a porte cochere producing a theatrical sense of entry into another era. Most of the hotel continues along a low unobtrusive profile.

Indigenous natural materials with subtle color gradations that change with the desert light and seasons were used for exterior finishing. Stone walls, the palm-lined entry drive and picturesque walkways define the resort as a casually elegant oasis.

The elegant silk and brocade
European-style interiors of the lobby.

In true Ritz style, the hotel's public
areas are warm and richly appointed.

HOTEL COMPANY
Ritz-Carlton Hotel Company
ARCHITECTURE
Wimberly Allison Tong & Goo
INTERIOR DESIGN
Frank Nicholson
PHOTOGRAPHY
Berger / Conser

# Royal York Hotel

*TORONTO, CANADA*

Rich fabrics of tapestry and velvet
adorn the newly-renovated Royal York
Hotel.

At the time the Royal York Hotel opened in 1929, it was the largest hotel in the British empire. Today its 1,400 rooms, seven restaurants, four bars and two floors of ballrooms have been lovingly restored to its original elegance.

The intent was to do a minor ''face lift'' until original photographs were discovered. It was at this point that the owners, Canadian Pacific Hotels, agreed that a major renovation and restoration was in order. Much of the beautiful old travertine columns and walls had been covered and somewhat destroyed by the direct gluing of flexwood and heavy wood moldings. The other detail needing major renovation was lighting. Most of the beautiful decorative ceiling had been ''hidden'' by glaring light fixtures and therefore had gone unnoticed. The solution was to restore the original travertine, design custom chandeliers and wall sconces and remove obstructive ceiling light sources. The result is a return to elegance for this magnificent landmark hotel.

HOTEL COMPANY
Canadian Pacific Hotels & Resorts
INTERIOR DESIGN
Deborah Lloyd Forrest Associates
PHOTOGRAPHY
Mary Nichols

The magnificent lobby has been restored to include original travertine columns and walls, custom chandeliers and wall sconces and a beautifully-restored decorative ceiling.

# SAS Royal Hotel

*AMSTERDAM, THE NETHERLANDS*

North side facade showing three historical buildings which have been integrated in the design.

Although there seems to be a trend toward incorporating existing historical buildings into modern hotel facilities, this particular structure in Amsterdam posed several interesting design challenges.

The project is located in a part of old Amsterdam which consists of medieval and 18th century buildings which had great historical and monumental importance. The goal was to connect the build-ings on two sides of the street in such a way that guests did not experience cross-ing over from one part to the next and to integrate the existing historical buildings in the total complex in a harmonious and efficient manner. The third goal was to create a service basement due to the lim-ited prime ground floor area. The base-ment had to be made partially under the already existing monumental buildings.

The hotel consists of two blocks, and an existing large 18th century building on the south side of the street and a com-plex of new construction on the north. The two buildings are thereby connected by an underground lobby which incor-porates strong design features such as spiral staircases, floor cutouts and inven-tive lighting. A rotating art exhibit helps distract the view.

This new hotel has successfully and creatively woven historical and contemporary architecture into the fabric of the complex. The harmony of contrasts, which is a theme of the complex, is thus achieved throughout.

HOTEL COMPANY
SAS International Hotels
ARCHITECTURE
Boparai Associates B.V.
INTERIOR DESIGN
Christian Lundwall Architektkontor

Spiral staircase in floor cutouts
providing access between underground connection and ground level.

# St. Andrews Old Course Hotel

The ultimate golf experience must be to play the original, the place where it all began almost five centuries ago—the St. Andrews Old Course. And, where would you expect to stay other than the St. Andrews Old Course Hotel, newly renovated by the team of RTKL and Wilson & Associates.

Of course the design theme was to create an Old-World feel, but rather than imitate the traditional country house hotel, Wilson's group opted for a more genteel and comfortable space, with Scottish elements throughout. The idea was to introduce light into the spaces and orient the spectacular views to the outdoors.

The entry foyer off the motor court creates the first impression of the Old-World. The cool slate flooring is enhanced by the bisque color of the faux stone finish on the curved walls. A decorative frieze in the dome draws your attention immediately toward the clear skylight while rich tapestries and intricate iron table bases accent the space.

The entry foyer features bisque-colored scored faux stone and curved walls. Rich tapestry material and intricate iron table bases continue the Old-World theme.

The Conservatory provides deep, over-scaled furniture from which to enjoy the magnificent view.

The Conservatory is where to go to experience the 17th hole from an arm-chair perspective. This sun-filled room affords magnificent views. A trellis overlay enhances the sky blue ceiling with rounded coffer. A massive chandelier and upholstered pieces are generously scaled and covered in rich materials. Rattan highback chairs are pulled around and fitted with comfortable cushions. Here, the slate floors are enhanced by a hand-stenciled sisal rug.

Mahogany woods lightened with yew accents make up most of the guestrooms.

**ARCHITECTURE**
RTKL Associates
**INTERIOR DESIGN**
Wilson & Associates
**PHOTOGRAPHY**
Scott McDonald for Hedrich-Blessing

Guestrooms too are warm and cozy with traditional mahogany woods lightened with accents. The key here is comfort from the lounge chairs to the carpeting. Artwork in the rooms includes reproductions of original prints of St. Andrews botanicals in gilt wood frames and Scottish landscape prints.

The cozy guestroom features a Scottish hydrangea print on the dust skirt and drapery.

# Hotel St. Raphael

*HAMBURG, GERMANY*

On the occasion of the European Community Tourist Year 1991, the Danish hotel supplier X-Design Studio and the Swiss textile manufacturer Mira-X joined to promote a unique design challenge. Ten architects, designers and stylists were asked to design one bedroom each in the new wing of the St. Raphael Hotel in Hamburg. No limits were set as the designers were given a free hand in choosing furniture, materials, colors, lighting, etc.

The outcome has been well-received and provides an interesting new dimension to hotel design for Hamburg. These designer rooms are very much in demand and they will surely not be forgotten for some time.

HOTEL COMPANY
Best Western International Inc.

Design as an experiment by Lilian
Pedersen, Textile Designer, Arhus,
Denmark.

# Sheraton Moana Surfrider

*Honolulu, Hawaii, USA*

Six and one half years of research, planning and design and construction went into the historic restoration of the Sheraton Moana Surfrider. Because there were no architectural drawings of the original hotel, the project architectural team was forced to rely upon old photographs to recreate original designs and to determine scale, proportion and placement of design features. According to the designers, one of the main challenges was to recreate a large-scale wooden structure, replicating construction methods and materials not used for several decades. One prominent feature throughout the hotel is the extensive re-establishment of exterior and interior millwork to the correct scale and proportions of the original structure.

*The Hotel once again revels in the graciousness of a resort hotel in 1918.*

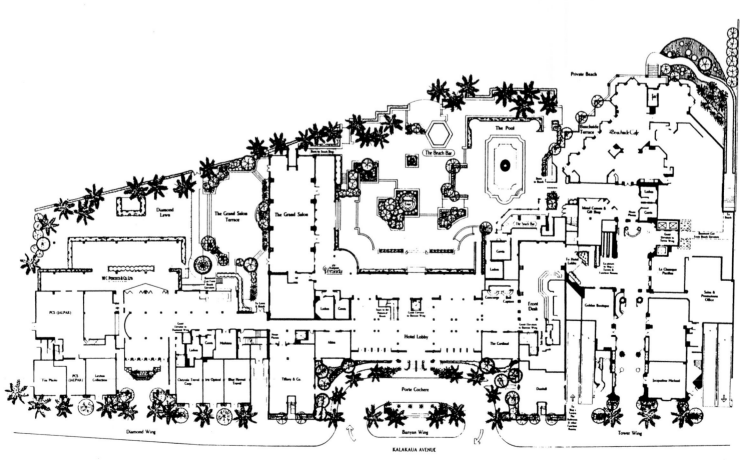

The intricate millwork had to be recreated from old photographs.

HOTEL COMPANY
Sheraton
ARCHITECTURE
Virginia D. Murison/
Chapman Desai Sakata
PHOTOGRAPHY
© 1990 Christopher Irion

# Stouffer Harborplace Hotel

*Baltimore, Maryland, USA*

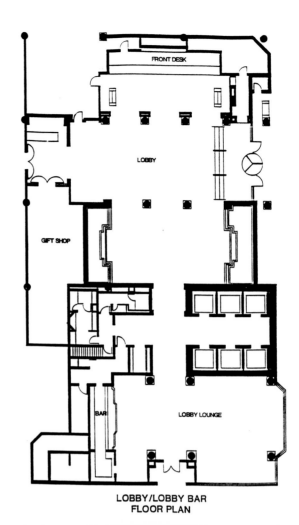

LOBBY/LOBBY BAR
FLOOR PLAN

With a bustling new waterfront in Baltimore, the lobby of the Stouffer Harborplace Hotel has become an active part of this multi-use complex.

The designers wanted to create a lobby and lobby bar that would accommodate the bustling crowd without intimidating hotel guests. The solution was to create a strong T-axis to channel the pedestrian traffic flow and create quiet cul-de-sacs of bar and lobby seating. Even the delightful interplay of water features with seating nearby add to the calming nature of the lobby.

The rich mahogany paneling and columns speak of a residential influence, while the marble flooring, beveled mirrors and granite cladding speak of the public and enormous scope of the building as a whole.

HOTEL COMPANY
Stouffer
INTERIOR DESIGN
Harper Design
PHOTOGRAPHY
Jaime Ardiles-Arce

The lobby bar features a club-like atmosphere. It is located adjacent to the lobby without being divorced from the active lobby atmosphere.

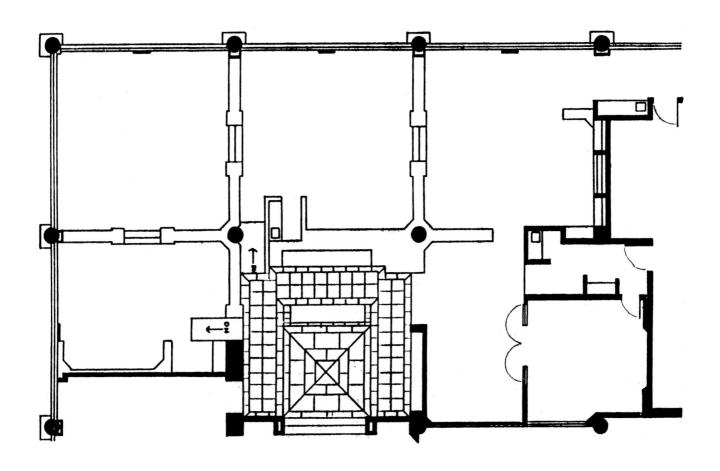

# Stouffer Stanford Court Hotel

*SAN FRANCISCO, CALIFORNIA, USA*

The new Presidential Suite at the
Stanford Court features traditional
furnishings with a decidedly oriental
flavor.

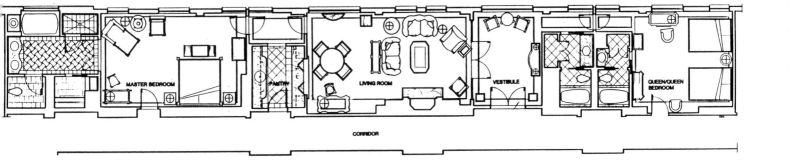

MASTER BEDROOM    PANTRY    LIVING ROOM    VESTIBULE    QUEEN/QUEEN BEDROOM

CORRIDOR

The elegant marble bath in the Presidential Suite provides soakers with a luxurious view of the city.

The Stouffer Stanford Court Hotel makes a statement, even in a city well-known for its elegant hotels. When it was ready for an upgrade and remodel, Harper Design was called upon.

One of the biggest design challenges came from converting a little-used meeting space to a luxurious Presidential Suite. The design theme was to create a luxury environment which reflected the international nature of the city, especially its ties with the countries of the Pacific Rim.

The room's dimensions, an ill-proportioned rectangle at best, created the first challenge. Then, hiding the plumbing ducts proved to be more than interesting, but ultimately what was created was a comfortable yet elegant space befitting this old gem of a hotel. French doors were added for sparkle, mirrors were placed strategically, a vestibule was created and a luxurious carpet was added to encourage the extension of space.

**G**reat care was taken with the master bathroom to maximize the feeling of luxury. The spacious double shower has a marble floor and from the bath can be seen a spectacular view of the city. Extensive use of wood, mirror and marble recall luxury liner cabins of the past.

**T**he millwork, marble and mirror detailing is traditional—all appropriate for an historic building in the ''city of landmarks.''

HOTEL COMPANY
*Stouffers*
**INTERIOR DESIGN**
*Harper Design Company*
**PHOTOGRAPHY**
*Sally Painter*

# Vista Marquette Hotel

*MINNEAPOLIS, MINNESOTA, USA*

Intradesign's approach to creating a unique interior design statement at the Marquette began with the award-winning Phillip Johnson-designed building completed in 1972. Richard Mayhew, Director of Design at Intradesign displayed uncommonly creative versatility to this inspiring project.

The exterior of the Marquette provided clean, contemporary lines allowing the interiors to add both contemporary and classical elements. Marble and granite surfaces, polished metal trim and glazing reflect an intimate and residential character. The furnishings, created by crisp, tailored lines of upholstered seating in varied textures and custom hand-knotted carpets over marble floors compliment the overall design theme. Original designs for seating and casegoods provide a signature look for the hotel suggesting the warmth of being in a fine and elegant home.

ARCHITECTURE
Shea Architects, Inc.
INTERIOR DESIGN
Intradesign, Inc. — Richard Mayhew,
Wendy Lumsden, David Peebles
PHOTOGRAPHY
Klein & Wilson

The use of classic architectural accents and art blend with contemporary furnishings to create a visually interesting design atmosphere.

The classic yet softly-contemporary furnishings of the Marquette focus on an eclectic combination of textures and styles.

Strategically placed feature art and artifacts exhibit works of local and regional artists.

# Waterfront Hilton

*Huntington Beach, California, USA*

The lower lobby features a lush tropical setting with terra cotta pavers accented with travertine. Casual wicker chairs are upholstered in light pastel fabrics.

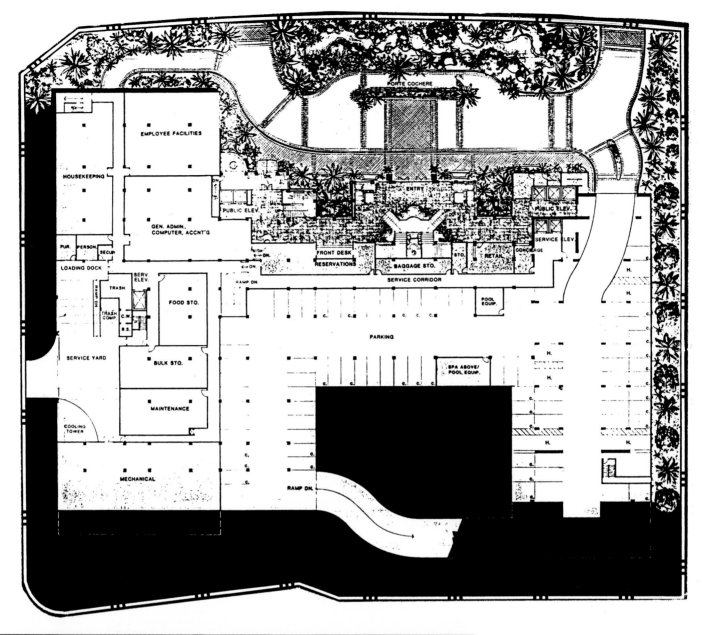

Just south of Los Angeles on the Pacific Coast Highway sits the Waterfront Hilton, part of a 50-acre destination resort that is the first phase of a major revitalization of Huntington Beach. The casual, timeless style of this 300-room hotel's contemporary Mediterranean architecture is well-suited to the beachfront property.

A small lobby bar comfortably accommodates guests who want to sit and take in the view of the pool

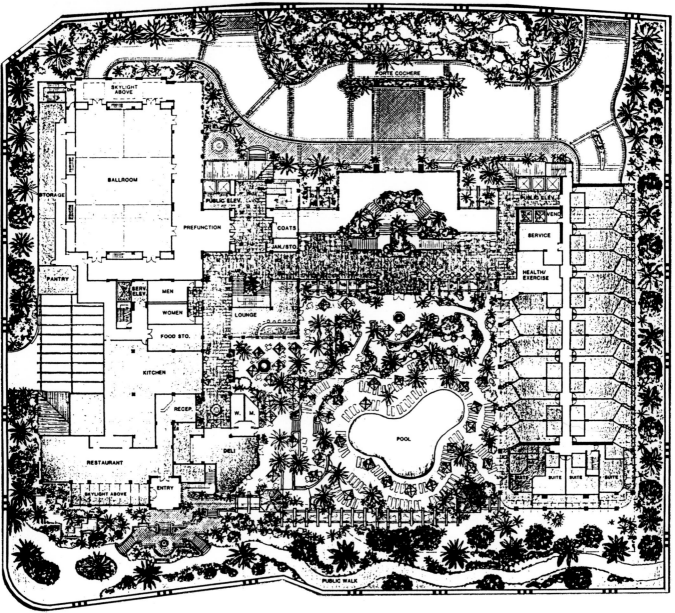

The lower lobby of the hotel has no views, so the tropical effect of the plant-scape plays a major role in creating ties to the resort ambience of the rest of the hotel. Terra cotta pavers with travertine accents provide the footing for casual wicker chairs and upholstered furnishings in light pastel colors. Gentle archways, decorative columns and chandeliers add interest to the lobby. Guests ascend the marble staircase to reach the upper lobby. Furnished with a Mediterranean flair, furnishings in this lobby are upholstered in beige leather or subtle coral prints. Bleached wood finishes, pale walls and arched windows without draperies keep the feeling light and airy.

Marble accents and a color scheme of soft mauves, beiges and greens highlight the guestrooms. Natural wood finishes and hand-painted floral canvas bedspreads add to the comfortable bedroom scheme.

HOTEL COMPANY
Robert Mayer Corp.
ARCHITECTURE
Wimberly Allison Tong & Goo
INTERIOR DESIGN
Concepts 4, Inc.
PHOTOGRAPHY
Berger/Conser

# The Westin Hotel

*INDIANAPOLIS, INDIANA, USA*

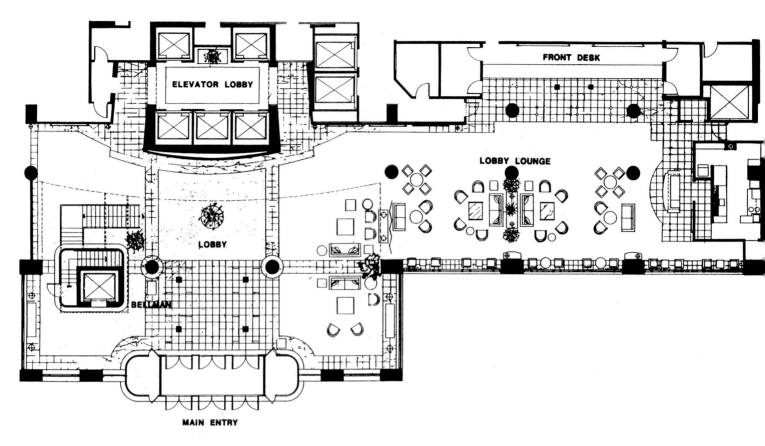

*Classic, contemporary and post modern designs create the elegant lobby.*

**D**esigning a grand contemporary hotel in the heart of a somewhat conservative Midwestern metropolis, without alienating locals while still welcoming a diverse guest base is indeed a challenge. But add to that the challenge of creating an upscale Westin with furnishings durable enough to withstand very heavy hospitality use with easy maintenance and you have the challenge faced by FORMA design. "We wanted to position it as the premier hotel in the city in terms of size, finish and appearance," said senior designer Robert Clark. "It had to give the city a sophistication that wasn't there, yet still appeal to local clientele."

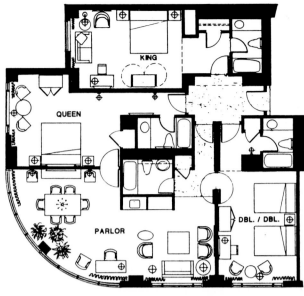

Because the property is located in a prime location, right in the main square, adjacent to the Hoosier Dome, capital building and convention center, the Westin is largely tied to convention business—a market that attracts guests from every level of taste and sophistication.

FORMA chose custom-designed furnishings to achieve elegance and richness at modest cost. A combination of traditional and contemporary furnishings, polished marble flooring, bleached wood moldings, glazed terra-cotta walls, richly detailed millwork and elegantly patterned wool carpeting creates a welcome, residential feel.

**HOTEL COMPANY**
Westin Hotels
**ARCHITECTURE**
Lamson & Condon, Inc.
**INTERIOR DESIGN**
FORMA
**PHOTOGRAPHY**
John Vaughan, Russell MacMasters
& Associates

Classic elegance and contemporary
design position this property as the
premier hotel in Indianapolis.

# The Westin Hotel

*SAN FRANCISCO AIRPORT, CALIFORNIA, USA*

The unique custom registration pods provide travelers with a new check-in experience.

For weary air travelers, the Westin Hotel at the San Francisco Airport provides a surprisingly quiet and cozy haven, usually found in small resort hotels. This 393-room property resists large interior and conference vistas in trade for more intimate, residential spaces. Jet lagged guests register at several freestanding pods instead of the traditional front desk. From the reception, guests can immediately absorb the intimate residential feel of the hotel.

The main lobby provides weary travelers with more of a residential feel than that of an airport hotel.

This unique airport hotel leaves business travelers thinking they have just vacationed in a fine resort.

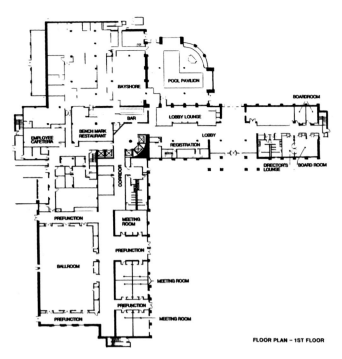

FLOOR PLAN – 1ST FLOOR

The overall style is cosmopolitan and eclectic, reflecting the sophistication of the Bay Area. Against the backdrop of soft neutrals, a mix of custom-designed contemporary and traditional furnishings are peppered with a special collection of Asian artifacts both antique and contemporary.

**HOTEL COMPANY**
Westin Hotels
**ARCHITECTURE**
Leo A. Daly
**INTERIOR DESIGN**
FORMA
**PHOTOGRAPHY**
John Vaughan, Russell MacMasters and Associates (all photos except guestrooms)
Chris Eden, Eden Arts (guestrooms)

# The Westin South Coast Plaza

*ORANGE COUNTY, CALIFORNIA, USA*

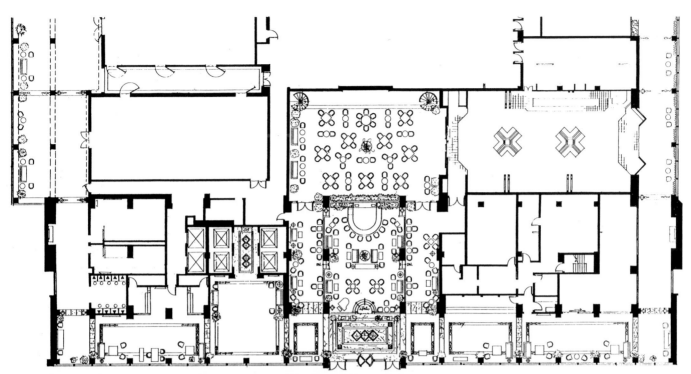

Charged with creating an economical yet highly marketable end product to a discerning California audience, the designers devoted a considerable amount of time and attention to space planning (particularly in the public areas) and to specifying high-quality materials and finishes. Most of the interior design work was custom-designed in order to achieve elegance and richness at moderate cost.

The lobby and lobby lounge were designed to reflect the upscale, urban sophistication of the hotel's Orange County location. Columns and beams were added, creating a series of intimate gathering spaces. At the same time, these architectural elements also provide opportunities for the display of fine artwork which has become an integral part of the design. Marble floors and columns, custom woven carpeting, beveled glass paneling, contemporary-furnishings with classical lines and a soft, monochromatic color scheme combine to create a rich, understated California elegance.

The lobby lounge combines contrasting textures of leather, tapestry and silk in warm colors of travertine, grays and soft pastels.

HOTEL COMPANY
Westin Hotels & Resorts
INTERIOR DESIGN
FORMA
PHOTOGRAPHY
Milroy / McAleer Photography

# Williamsburg Inn

*Williamsburg, Virginia, USA*

English country scenes from the 19th century adorn the walls in this guestroom.

The 19th century classical design of the Williamsburg Inn was intentionally designed to contrast with the 18th century architecture of the area. The hotel's clean sense of classic style and balance has been carefully incorporated into the interior design.

From its beginnings, the Williamsburg Inn has embodied the studied understatement and refinement of its earliest benefactors, Mr. and Mrs. John D. Rockefeller, Jr. They were determined that the Inn would be ''absolutely unlike a hotel, but rather like a private home-away-from-home.''

Among the ongoing design challenges at the Inn is the ability to secure materials and furnishings that are accurate to the period and a high level of quality. Since none of the 102 guestrooms are alike, the challenge becomes a full-time opportunity for the Inn's own in-house design studio, staffed by designers who are required to have a background in period design.

HOTEL COMPANY
Colonial Williamsburg Hotel Properties
ARCHITECTURE
Perry, Shaw & Hepburn
INTERIOR DESIGN
Susan L. Winther

Characterized by darker colors and
heavier fabrics, the main entrance
lobby is shown in its winter scheme

This guestroom was the 1989 American Hotel & Motel Association Gold Key Award for excellence in interior design. The room features all original artwork.

# INDEX

## ARCHITECTURE

## PHOTOGRAPHY

## INTERIOR DESIGN

# HOTELS